Spaces and Politics of Motherhood

Spaces and Politics of Motherhood

Kate Boyer

ROWMAN &
LITTLEFIELD
————INTERNATIONAL
London • New York

Published by Rowman & Littlefield International Ltd.
Unit A, Whitacre Mews, 26–34 Stannary Street, London SE11 4AB
www.rowmaninternational.com

Rowman & Littlefield International Ltd. is an affiliate of Rowman & Littlefield
4501 Forbes Boulevard, Suite 200, Lanham, Maryland 20706, USA
With additional offices in Boulder, New York, Toronto (Canada), and Plymouth (UK)
www.rowman.com

British Library Cataloguing in Publication Data
A catalogue record for this book is available from the British Library

ISBN: HB 978-1-78660-307-4
         PB 978-1-78660-308-1

Library of Congress Cataloging-in-Publication Data Available
ISBN: 978-1-78660-307-4 (cloth : alk. paper)
ISBN: 978-1-78660-308-1 (pbk : alk. paper)
ISBN: 978-1-78660-309-8 (electronic)

Contents

Introduction

This book is about the spaces and politics of early motherhood. As feminist theorist Hannah Stark observes, 'Politics is about how we imagine and enact collective life' (Stark, 2017: 99). Herein I explore the politics of how early motherhood is lived and imagined, focusing on the first year after the birth of a first child, examining the kinds of experiences and changes that can take place during that time.

Like many books, this one was motivated in part by personal experience – in this case my experience of becoming a mother in 2008. Giving birth nine months after moving to the United Kingdom from the United States made me especially interested in the differences in birth and parenting cultures between these two countries. From the cost neutrality of having a baby 'on the National Health Service' to the significantly longer maternity leaves in the UK to the more robust landscape of parenting advocacy in the form of parenting charity, the NCT (National Childbirth Trust), certain things jumped out at me regarding differences in birth and parenting cultures between the two countries. This included some surprises regarding the respective birth and parenting cultures in these two places, for example, the fact that despite its longer and more generous maternity allowance, the UK has lower rates of breastfeeding duration than the US. This is surprising given the respective levels of institutional support between the two countries and suggests that there are important features of how motherhood happens 'on the ground' in spaces of lived practice that can supersede policy initiatives.

This is a book about how motherhood happens on the ground, in spaces of everyday life focusing on the embodied practices and lived experiences of becoming a mother. Empirically this book is based on the experiences of mothers in the UK and the US gleaned through research conducted over a period of nine years. This included participant observation, ethnographic

1

work, survey work and interviews with thirty-one new mothers in London and South East England undertaken between 2008 and 2016; thematic analysis of policy texts from the UK and the US; and textual analysis of entries in online parenting discussion groups and blogs in the UK and US.[1] Conceptually I engage themes of embodiment, relationality, affect and materiality. Empirically I explore such questions as the role of space and place in emergent understandings of maternal subjectivity; becoming mobile with a small baby; the embodied socio-spatial politics of infant feeding (focusing on breastfeeding); and the politics of some of the new ways care-work is being enfolded within wage-work. I hope this book might find audiences in disciplines of geography, anthropology, nursing and midwifery, women's studies, cultural studies, psychology, science and technology studies as well as sociology and among upper-level undergraduate students in relevant fields and interested general readers.

I would suggest that given the broad cultural resemblances between the UK, US and Commonwealth countries, there will be resonances between the arguments I make herein and the experiences of women in other cultural contexts. However, this book does not purport to give any 'universal truths' about motherhood. Experiences of motherhood vary tremendously across time and space and also differ *within* any given cultural context by intersecting factors of class, race/ethnicity, age, sexual orientation, gender identity and other vectors of social differentiation that structure advantage and disadvantage.[2] What this means is that experiences of motherhood are highly differentiated and occur through dual prisms of both one's cultural context and one's social position/location within that culture.[3] As Patricia Collins noted in her essay 'Shifting the Center: Race, Class and Feminist Theorizing about Motherhood' (1994) about motherhood in the 1990s US: 'For women of color, the subjective experience of mothering/motherhood is inextricably linked to the sociocultural concern of racial ethnic communities – one does not exist without the other' (Collins, 1994: 47). I would suggest that this observation holds a wider truth for the power of culture and social location to shape maternal experience.

The experiences of motherhood and forms of maternal becoming, which I consider here, are thus not universal but particular, culturally situated and context-dependent. Although my data set reflects a degree of both ethno-cultural and socio-economic diversity (discussed in the following chapter summaries and in more detail in the chapters themselves), the lion's share of data on which this study is based reflect the experiences of white, British, non-poor, heterosexual, cisgender, able-bodied mothers. As such this analysis of motherhood reflects a disproportionately privileged set of mothering experiences. Relatedly, my own status as the mother of a young child while undertaking the research and writing of this book also shaped the narrative in myriad ways. My experiences and memories influenced the kinds of questions I asked and how interviews unfolded. At the same time, as a white, heterosexual, cisgender woman with a professional job, my own social position is one of relative privilege. These factors shaped my experience of mothering, as well as shaping (and constraining) how I accessed and understood the stories and knowledge of others.

As well, I would like to say a few words about my decision to focus on mothers in this book. I recognise the important physical and emotional work that fathers do and believe fathers can parent just as well as mothers.[4] But, after Aitken (2000), Dermott (2008), Doucet (2006) and others, I also recognise that fathering is different from mothering and cannot be distilled down into mothering. I am excited by the prospect of more gender-equitable approaches to caring for young children from what they are currently. At present, however, structural factors of (much) longer maternity leave relative to paternity leave in the UK;[5] the stubborn gap in male and female wage rates throughout the wage-labour market; and cultural norms which continue to posit childcare as 'women's work' mean that the care of young children continues to be done principally by women in both the UK and the US (and beyond). In the research underpinning this book it was mothers who were doing the majority of childcare, had the time and inclination to be interviewed post-birth and took time to share and discuss issues important to them online.[6] These factors led to the decision to focus on mothering in this work.

CONCEPTUAL FRAMING

Conceptually this book builds on existing scholarship by deepening our understanding of motherhood as a spatial practice. I extend existing conceptual work by exploring the ways maternal practice occurs in and through engagements with the non-human. This engagement is informed by the move across the humanities and social sciences over the past decade to unseat human subjects as the primary ontological focus of inquiry (posthumanism). While not abandoning human agency, in this work I seek to expand our understanding of the myriad different agentic forces that shape how motherhood is experienced. Building on existing scholarship, I explore what new kinds of understandings of motherhood might emerge through a greater attunement to interactions between mothers and the various more-than-human forces with which they interface in the course of parenting.

Scholarship has explored the power of expert discourses in shaping maternal practice (Brown, 2016), as well as the role of partners and peer supporters (Rollins et al., 2016), infants (Holt, 2013) and others in shaping how motherhood happens. *Spaces and Politics of Motherhood* extends this work by considering some of the more-than-human forces at play in shaping early motherhood, including that of matter, the maternal body and even strangers, together with an analysis of the efforts of mothers themselves to draw forth more enabling forms of maternal practice. Through engagement with Deleuzian, feminist and new materialist philosophy I explore early motherhood through concepts of materiality, material agency, assemblage theory and becoming. I advance a concept of motherhood as an endeavour of *distributed agency*, highlighting the multiple forms of agency at work within parenting assemblages, including that of the more-than-human.

In recent years an increasing number of geographers have begun to engage with scholarship coming out of contemporary feminist theory as a way to analyse the spatial politics of materiality, embodiment and ways of understanding the world beyond the medium of texts. Rachael Colls (2012: 434) has outlined what she casts as a 'terrain of shared concern' between feminist theory and nonrepresentational geography via the work of Elisabeth Grosz (1994, 2005), Rosi Braidotti (1994, 2003) and Luce Irigaray (2004). Relatedly, in their work on placentas Colls and Maria Fannin present a way of working which synthesises both feminist and nonrepresentational approaches in their analysis of the placenta as a mediating force between the body of the mother and that of the foetus (Colls and Fannin, 2013).

Building on this, a key area of scholarship for geographers and others seeking to engage themes of practice, materiality and embodiment in ways that do not ignore social power relations (e.g., those of gender, race, class and sexual orientation) is the body of theory known as the *New Materialism* (Alaimo and Hekman, 2008; Barad, 2007; Braidotti, 2002; Colebrook, 2008; Coole and Frost, 2010). Composed of scholarship cutting across the humanities, philosophy and the natural sciences, new materialist social theory is concerned with creating analyses which take seriously both discourse and other forms of representation, as well as the nonrepresentational, including matter, affect and emotion (Alaimo and Hekman, 2008; Coole and Frost, 2010; Van der Tuin and Dolphijn, 2012). Drawing on a long tradition of feminist scholarship, scholars working in the new materialist tradition seek to give more analytical attention to the politics of materiality and embodied practice as well as sharpen analysis of how practice and representation relate to one another. As Coole and Frost (2010: 2) put it, 'Corporeality (is) . . . crucial for a materialist theory of politics or agency', while feminist theoretician Hannah Stark similarly calls for the need to 'focus on the lived practices that reveal the various ways in which subjects are embodied, located and connected' (Stark, 2017: 66). This orientation harmonises nicely with work in contemporary feminist geography which emphasises issues of embodiment and lived practice.

The New Materialism also draws on feminist and Deleuzoguattarian conceptualisations of subjectivity as an ongoing process of becoming, highlighting the role of matter in those processes (Braidotti, 2002: 8; Deleuze and Guattari, 2004). In the tradition of Haraway, Whatmore, Colls and Fannin and others, new materialist philosophy seeks to destabilise firm conceptual boundaries between bodies and matter by attending to what Karan Barad terms 'agential intra-action', referring to the ways that meanings are produced *relationally*, in and through the relations between phenomena (Barad, 2007: 33). As Stark puts it, envoking a Deleuzian frame, 'The body cannot be thought of as individual, bounded or coherent because it is constituted fundamentally by the connections it enters into', noting further that 'these connections do not discriminate between the human and the non-human' (Stark, 2017: 75). Informed by this theoretical frame, *Spaces and Politics of Motherhood* develops a conceptualisation of early motherhood as a coming-together of multiple forms of agency encompassing human, material, cultural and biological actors and actants. As such it extends cross-disciplinary work on motherhood as well as advancing fields of feminist, social and cultural geography, feminist studies, sociology and anthropology, encompassing both policy and social experience within the two cultural contexts of the UK and US. Having outlined my main conceptual frames I will now turn to discuss the empirical scholarship on which this book builds before moving on to provide an outline of each chapter.

LITERATURE REVIEW

There are obviously a large number of books across many disciplines on the subject of motherhood (as there should be!), and it is beyond the scope of this literature review to offer a comprehensive view of this rich field. I will therefore focus on the work that pertains most directly to the topics and themes addressed here. Over the past thirty years understandings of motherhood in the Anglo-US context have been strongly influenced by the work of Adrienne Rich on how motherhood is shaped and constrained by patriarchy (Rich, 1995); Sarah Ruddick's work on motherhood as a practice or kind of 'doing' rather than a passive or stable state of being (Ruddick, 1989); and Sharon Hays's work on how mothers are expected to be both endlessly self-less towards their children and also intensively engaged in the wage-labour market ('intensive' mothering) (Hays, 1998). This book owes a debt to their scholarship.

Spaces and Politics of Motherhood is also situated within a rich history of scholarship on motherhood and space that has emerged in geography over the past thirty years. This scholarship has highlighted such issues as the spatial confinement and isolation of mothers over the life course (Bowlby, 1990); the impact of childcare responsibilities (including the school-run) on labour-market participation and career progression (England, 1996; Schwanen et al., 2008; TUC, 2013); and the symbolic power of mothers' presence in and use of public space, including as activists (Naples, 1998; Spain, 2001; Wilson, 1992). Analyses of early parenthood (from birth to roughly age one) have begun to garner attention through scholarship on the experiences of lesbian mothers (Luzia, 2010); the role of the Internet in the formation of maternal identity (Longhurst, 2013; Madge and O'Connor, 2005); how mothering and fathering intersect with other forms of identity (Aitken, 1998, 2000; McDowell et al., 2006); the way contemporary parenting is shaped by narratives of risk (Holloway, 1998; McDowell et al., 2006; Pain, 2006; Talbot, 2013); and the role of infant agency within parenting assemblages (Holt, 2013). *Spaces and Politics of Motherhood* both builds on and extends this work in ways that will be outlined in more detail in each substantive chapter.

A number of books have also been published in feminist geography which include motherhood as part of their focus. These include *Full Circles: Geographies of Women over the Life Course* (Katz and Monk, 1993); *Who Will Mind the Baby? Geographies of Childcare and Working Mothers* (England, 1996); *Life's Work: Geographies of Social Reproduction* (Mitchell et al., 2004); *Families Apart: Migrant Mothers and the Conflicts of Labor and Love* (Pratt, 2012); and *Maternities: Gender, Bodies and Space* (Longhurst, 2008). Each of these works has brought significant advances in geographic analyses of motherhood and raised the visibility of motherhood and parenthood as foci for geographers. *Full Circles* explored the experiences of women through the life course across a range of different cultural contexts while *Who Will Mind the Baby?* investigated mothers' experiences of combining childcare with wage-work in the 1990s. *Life's Work* engaged questions of identity and everyday practice through empirical chapters on education, nationalism, justice and modernity. *Families Apart* explored conceptual and political concerns about parenting and political economy via the experiences of geographically ruptured parenting on the part of Filipina nannies in Canada. *Maternities* explored pregnancy and birth from the perspectives of pornography, cross-species breastfeeding and the role of the Internet in identity-work for mothers in New Zealand.

Spaces and Politics of Motherhood differentiates itself from each of these works through its UK/US focus; its temporal focus on the period of the first year post-birth; and by engaging questions of materiality, affect and the more-than-human. It builds on existing work in the field by offering an analysis of common, day-to-day experiences of motherhood which, while particular, are also experiences to which a plurality of mothers can likely relate.

Spaces and Politics of Motherhood bears further affinities with a number of titles outside the discipline of geography on topics of motherhood. These include *Motherhood and Space* (Hardy and Wiedmer, 2005); *The Demands of Motherhood* (Smyth, 2012); *Consuming Motherhood* (Taylor et al., 2004); *Making Modern Mothers* (Thomson et al., 2011); *Making Sense of Motherhood: A Narrative Approach* (Miller, 2005); and *Twenty-First Century Motherhood* (O'Reilly, 2010). These will be addressed in turn. The book with closest empirical connection to this one is *Motherhood and Space*, an edited edition with contributions from scholars across the humanities and social sciences on pregnancy, birth and motherhood across different cultural contexts. However, despite the thematic similarity there is very little empirical or conceptual overlap between that book and this one.

The Demands of Motherhood considers motherhood from the perspective of pragmatism, expressive individualism and normative complexity based on interviews with mothers in Ireland and the US. Though an important contribution to the field, its conceptual framing and empirical focus are significantly different from this one. *Consuming Motherhood* shares an empirical focus with chapter 2 (on prams), and I have drawn important insights from several of the chapters in this volume. However, the conceptual approaches differ as my analysis is not based on consumption but rather on the New Materialism. I have likewise drawn a number of insights from the influential book *Making Modern Mothers* although empirically this book differs from that one in that it focuses on the period from pregnancy to birth (whereas birth is where the empirical focus of this book begins).

Making Sense of Motherhood similarly makes a valuable contribution to motherhood scholarship, but it only shares an empirical concern with one chapter of *Spaces and Politics of Motherhood* (on identity in early motherhood) and does not share the same conceptual approach. *Twenty-First Century Motherhood* offers a fascinating sampler of scholarship across a wide range of cultural contexts and covers a wide range of conceptual themes. These include engagements with the new landscape of technology relating to maternity and childbirth, queer parenting, experiences of raising transgender children, as well as mothers from minority backgrounds in the US (including Chicana, Muslim and lesbian mothers) who work in activist capacities to challenge discrimination. I have drawn on this work where I explore mothers' activism around rights to the city (in chapter 5) and share with it a desire to advance understanding about some of the other forms agency at play in shaping maternal experience.

Moreover, like *Maternities* and *Motherhood and Space*, each of the above works looks at motherhood in the round, typically considering pregnancy, birth and early motherhood together (or in the case of *Making Modern Mothers*, the period up to birth only). *Spaces and Politics of Motherhood* further differentiates itself from each of these works not only by bringing substantially new theoretical concerns to the understanding of motherhood but also through its focus on spatial practices in the first year post-birth, none of which any of these titles spend significant time on.

As well, *Spaces and Politics of Motherhood* also shares affinities with a number of books and articles on infant feeding. This scholarship will be discussed in greater detail in chapters 4 and 5, and again, this too is a massive field encompassing scholarship across the social sciences, humanities and biological sciences, and it is not my intention to offer a comprehensive summary of it here. That said, it is worth highlighting some of the key titles with which this work shares conceptual terrain. These include *Breastfeeding Uncovered: Who Really Decides How We Feed Our Babies* (Brown, 2016); *Nighttime Breastfeeding: An American Cultural Dilemma* (Tomori, 2014); *Breastwork: Rethinking Breastfeeding* (Bartlett, 2005); *Mother's Milk: Breastfeeding Controversies in American Culture* (Hausman, 2003); *Beyond Health, Beyond Choice: Breastfeeding Constraints and Realities* (Smith et al., 2012); and *Ethnographies of Breastfeeding: Cultural Contexts and Confrontations* (Cassidy and El Tom, 2015).

While Amy Brown highlights the need to support women trying to breast-feed, underscoring the damaging effects of messages that breastfeeding should be hidden and making a case for the fact that it is the job of society as a whole to help remove barriers to women seeking to breastfeed in the UK (Brown, 2016), Cecilia Tomori offers a careful analysis of the relationship between successful breastfeeding and co-sleeping through her anthropological study of new families in the Upper Midwestern US (Tomori, 2014).

Alison Bartlett's seminal book *Breastwork* approaches breastfeeding from a literary/cultural studies perspective, showing how knowledge about breastfeeding is mediated by expert discourses and shaped by media and other forms of cultural representation in the Australian case. While covering similar issues as Brown's work, I take analysis in a new direction by drawing out the micro-politics of women's experiences of breastfeeding in public in the contemporary UK. Likewise, while concentrating on the same time period of early motherhood, this work differs from Tomori's by also considering experiences of early motherhood in the UK.

Although covering similar issues as chapter 4, *Breastwork* differs in conceptual framing as well as geographical context. Similarly, while Bernise Hausman's foundational book *Mother's Milk* was instrumental in the framing of the ideas behind this book, this work differs from that one in its geographical focus. *Beyond Health, Beyond Choice* offers a range of instructive essays proposing a conceptual *rapprochement* between feminist theory and breastfeeding advocacy. While there is topical overlap with chapters 4 and 6 of this book, *Beyond Health, Beyond Choice* differs in its focus on public health providers, while *Ethnographies of Breastfeeding* differs in its global approach to experiences of breastfeeding.

In addition to the aforementioned books, *Spaces and Politics of Motherhood* owes a debt to the rich array of published articles on breastfeeding. Regarding social experiences of breastfeeding in the cultural context of the UK (as discussed in chapters 4 and 5), the works of Fiona Dykes, Sally Dowling, Dawn Leeming, Aimee Grant, Lucilla Newell and Rachael Pain have been particularly useful in shaping this narrative. While Lucilla Newell has usefully suggested the concept of the assemblage as a way to think about breastfeeding (Newell, 2013), Fiona Dykes has argued for an interpretation of breastfeeding as embodied labour (Dykes, 2005). Dawn Leeming et al. have clearly and poignantly highlighted the role of feelings of shame and guilt for women for whom breastfeeding does not come easily (Leeming et al., 2013), and the work of Pain et al. has shown how breastfeeding outside the home was not common outside of London and more affluent urban neighbourhoods in the late 1990s in the UK, a trend which is still in evidence today (Pain et al., 2001).

Based on the seminal work of Cindy Stearns on women's experiences of breastfeeding in public in the US highlighting the sexualisation of women's breasts in this context (Stearns, 1999), Aimee Grant's analysis reveals the level of negative commentary that continues to be levelled at mothers who breastfeed in public by the readership of the UK's conservative tabloid and most-read newspaper, the *Daily Mail*. This work reveals how breastfeeding outside the home in the UK can be seen as exhibitionist and (remarkably) a sign of bad parenting (Grant, 2016). Similarly, as Dowling and Brown have shown, women in the UK who breastfeed for more than about a year (full-term or extended-term breastfeeding) face strong social stigma and opprobrium (Dowling and Brown, 2013). *Spaces and Politics of Motherhood* seeks to build on and extend this body of work.

In sum, *Spaces and Politics of Motherhood* brings something new to the fields of feminist geography, motherhood and breastfeeding studies. It analyses aspects of motherhood that are likely to be relatable for a plurality of mothers in Anglophone countries, focusing on a period of intense change (the first year post-birth) which has been underanalysed in the literature. Whereas most works consider either infant feeding or motherhood, I approach infant feeding as situated within practices of motherhood more generally (as I suggest it is experienced by mothers themselves). I also hope to bring a new and fresh conceptual framing, bringing in cutting-edge theoretical work across the social sciences and humanities on posthumanism, material agency and human–non-human relations. I develop an understanding of early motherhood from the prism of concepts of becoming, relationality and assemblages. Finally, *Spaces and Politics of Motherhood* is infused with the imagination and concerns of contemporary feminist and cultural geography and as such provides a different 'take' on motherhood than analyses from sociology, public health, nursing and midwifery, literary studies or other orientations.

CHAPTER OUTLINE

In the six topically focused chapters that follow, I highlight how the (some-times micro) politics of spatial practice can lead to more (and less) liberatory forms of motherhood. In broad outline chapters 1 through 3 explore maternal practice through theoretical engagements with posthumanism, the New Mate-rialism and Deleuzian theory, engaging concepts of becoming, assemblages and more-than-human agency. Chapters 4 through 6 shift focus to explore women's experiences of infant feeding through concepts of affect, public comfort (after Sara Ahmed) and neo-liberal motherhood. These chapters also expand outward to consider motherhood in the context of broader policy landscapes. Chapter 1, 'Maternal becomings: Space, time and subjectivity in early motherhood', considers early motherhood as a becoming through an analysis of some of the ways new mothers in the UK describe their experi-ences. Analysis is based on interviews with twenty new mothers in East London conducted in 2011 and 2012 and postings on the UK's most-used parenting website *mumsnet*. The interview data set was purposely selected to reflect social diversity and included both families from different socio-economic backgrounds and different racial and ethnic backgrounds, with eight of the twenty mothers being Afro-Caribbean and five white non-British. To put these data in a broader context, I also analysed reflections on new motherhood posted on non-password-protected chat boards on *mumsnet*, which receives ten million visits per month. Both of these data sets suggested ways in which the experience of new motherhood can entail a sense of dis-orientation or deterritorialisation from 'former selves'.

Based on an analysis of these data I suggest that early motherhood can be understood as a becoming, explaining this concept through the theoretical work of Braidotti, Deleuze and Guattari. Following from this I highlight the importance of *temporality* to understandings of maternal subjectivity both in the sense of change over time and a changed relationship *to* time. I approach motherhood as a dynamic process (rather than a fixed state) and suggest that this marks a conceptual innovation in how subjectivity typically appears in geography scholarship. Finally, I discuss the practice of journaling on the part of new mothers as a means to reflect on the implications of new mother-hood to (changing) sense of self, including by connecting to past and present selves, as well as to temporalities and spatialities beyond the (often tightly bound) time and space of early motherhood.

Chapters 2 and 3 explore the role of matter and material agency in maternal becomings. Chapter 2, 'Mothering with the world: Spatial practice, mobil-ity and material agency in maternal becomings', focuses on the material entanglements that occur in the course of becoming mobile with a small baby (e.g., with prams, built form and transport systems). Drawing on the interviews with mothers in East London described in chapter 1, in chapter 2 I use this data set to analyse the relationships between discourses of parenting and the material practices of journey-making. Analysing these data through conceptual work on the New Materialism and that of Deleuze and Guattari, I advance the concept of mother–baby assemblages as a way to understand mobile motherhood and consider the emotional and affective dimensions of parenting in public that can emerge through journey-making. I argue that the transition to motherhood occurs in part through entanglements with the more-than-human in the course of becoming mobile (including matter, affects, policies and built form). I further argue that approaching motherhood from the perspective of material entanglements advances our understanding of motherhood as a relational practice enacted through engagements with the more-than-human.

Chapter 3, 'Natureculture in the nursery: Lively breast milk, vibrant matter and the distributed agencies of infant feeding', expands our understanding of motherhood as a co-becoming with the non-human by exploring the multiple forms of agency involved in infant feeding. Public policy narratives (in the UK and beyond) are rife with the figure of mothers deciding how to feed their babies. Taking this a my starting point, chapter 3 expands this analytic frame to explore some of the other kinds of human and non-human agencies involved in infant feeding in addition to mothers, focusing on breastfeeding. Drawing on the New Materialism and scholarship within geography on the concept of naturecultures, this chapter advances our understanding of infant feeding by exploring the myriad bodily agencies at play in breastfeeding. Through an analysis of women's experiences of breastfeeding which do not go to plan (considering cases of mastitis and blocked ducts), I highlight the corporeal intra-actions that take place between mothers and their breasts, milk ducts and breast milk. Based on this I propose a posthumanist understanding of infant feeding which recognises the agentic force of breast milk and other bodily matter in shaping experiences of breastfeeding.

Chapter 4, 'Breastfeeding in public: Affect, public comfort and the agency of strangers', carries on from the theme of the distributed agencies of infant feeding to explore the role of strangers in mothers' efforts to breastfeed outside the home in the UK. *The UK has some of the lowest rates of breastfeeding in the world and has had for nearly the past fifty years* (McAndrew et al., 2012). Over 50% of UK mothers say they stopped breastfeeding before they wanted to, with most stopping within four weeks post-birth (McAndrew et al., 2012). This puts UK breastfeeding duration rates behind those of Canada, Australia, New Zealand and even the US (which has significantly less generous maternity allowance). Although the 'breast is best' public health message is thoroughly saturated in the UK, it is still a bottle-normative society. In many parts of the UK (and especially outside affluent neighbour-hoods in major cities), breastfeeding is uncommon and rarely seen.

Chapter 4 considers some of the factors that can shape women's experiences of breastfeeding outside the home in the weeks and months post-birth. Analysis is based on participant observation and interviews with eleven new mothers in Southampton, Hampshire, conducted in 2008–2009 together with my own experiences of breastfeeding in Southampton at this time. Analysis also draws on a forty-six-person survey of new mothers (also in Southampton), 180 postings about breastfeeding in public on *mumsnet* and a patent application for a 'portable lactation module'. I analyse these data through an engagement with the work of cultural theorist Sara Ahmed on public comfort and the comfort of strangers. Through this theoretical frame I argue that the 'limits of sociability' in public space in the UK can be marked affectively, through subtle (and sometimes unsubtle) signs of disapproval from members of the public. I submit that these negative affective atmospheres and expressions of disapproval can colour women's experiences of breastfeeding outside the home and feed into the decision to stop breastfeeding, even for women in areas where rates of breastfeeding are slightly higher than national averages. This chapter builds on my argument about early motherhood as a case of distributed agency by showing how breastfeeding functions as a relational practice in which the broader citizenry plays a role in structuring what kinds of spatial practices – and maternal becomings – are allowed or welcomed.

Chapters 2, 3 and 4 explore some of the myriad forms of agency shaping spatial practice and maternal becomings, including that of different kinds of matter and the broader public. Chapter 5, 'Mothers acting back: Claiming space through lactation advocacy', returns to mothers themselves to consider their capacity to resist or 'act back' against expectations of motherhood that are experienced as oppressive. Chapter 5 explores efforts to challenge limits placed on where maternal bodies and embodied care-work are allowed to take place. As argued in the previous chapter, discomfort about breastfeeding in public can be a factor shaping infant-feeding decisions and the decision to stop breastfeeding. With increased awareness of breast milk's health benefits in recent years, there has been a rise in efforts to make breastfeeding in public more socially acceptable in the UK, including through lactation advocacy (or 'lactivism'). This chapter considers breastfeeding advocacy through interviews with lactation activists, non-activist breastfeeding mothers and participant-observation at two public breastfeeding in England in 2009. Through an analysis of these data I argue that lactivism both makes explicit the political nature of maternal embodiment and embodied care-work and challenges extant ideas about rights to the city. I argue that lactivism can be understood as an effort to expand the boundaries of where embodied care-work is allowed to take place and can serve as a means to draw forth forms of motherhood that are more liberatory.

Finally, chapter 6, 'Combining care-work with wage-work: The changing policy landscape', follows on from the argument developed in chapter 5 about efforts to expand the range of places embodied care-work can occur, but shifts focus to explore the changing policy landscape relating to the combination of wage-work and care-work. I argue that in addition to matter, the body itself and members of the public, policy striates (or enables) particular kinds of maternal becomings. This chapter turns from the UK case to reflect on the possible future of combining wage-work with care-work through a consideration of provisions to protect the right to express breast milk in the wage-workplace passed in the US in 2011 (in the Patient Protection and Affordable Care Act).

This chapter explores the politics of how embodied care-work can – and might – be combined with wage-work and proposes a refinement to how wage-work/care-work relations are currently conceptualised. Expanding our understanding of working motherhood, I suggest that while this legislation challenges normative ideas of where embodied care-work can take place, it does so in a way that makes women's experiences of early motherhood more (rather than less) arduous. I make two arguments in this chapter. First, I argue that the 'goods' of this legislation are distributed unevenly, with women in professional jobs more likely to be able, in practical terms, to take up this right. In this way this legislation could exacerbate existing trends in the US which see more affluent mothers and babies gleaning more of the health benefits of breastfeeding as compared to younger, less affluent women and women of colour. In addition, I want to question 'how good' the potentials afforded by this legislation actually are. I argue that although intended to enable women to continue to breastfeed longer, this policy represents a form of work–life integration that is particularly burdensome for working mothers. I suggest that expectations relating to working motherhood in the contemporary US are being reshaped around the demands of neoliberalism, resulting in what can be thought of as 'neoliberal motherhood'. I conclude this chapter by highlighting how policy represents a way of combining wage-work and care-work that is not captured within existing conceptualisations and suggest that a reworking of theory in this area is needed to address ways in which embodied care-work is increasingly being enfolded within the time and space of wage-work. I conclude the book as a whole by offering a synthesis of themes explored herein relating to motherhood as a *political* and *spatial* practice that takes place with and through other aspects of the human and non-human world, flagging up directions for subsequent research.

Finally, like any book this one would never have been possible without the help and support of a great many people. First and foremost I would like to express my deep gratitude to everyone who participated in or helped facilitate the research on which this book is based. To all the new mothers who generously took time out from their already-full lives to share their reflections, insights, struggles and triumphs: I am in your debt. My thanks also go to the editorial team at Rowman & Littlefield International, including Martina O'Sullivan, Michael Watson, Holly Tyler and Natalie Bolderston for their enthusiasm and support for this project and all their help along the way, and Amy Walker for her editing support. Any/all remaining oversights or mistakes are wholly my own. I thank also Emma Healey at *mumsnet* on granting approval to include anonymised quotes from that website in this book and two anonymous reviewers who gave fantastic feedback and encouragement to this project at the proposal stage.

The research underpinning this book was enabled in part through various awards, and to these funders I express my thanks. The work on which chapter 6 is based was enabled by a travel grant to brainstorm ideas with Professor Rima Apple at the University of Wisconsin. I thank the World Universities Network for this opportunity, as well as Rima and her colleagues for their intellectual generosity. I would like to thank the University of Southampton's Department of Geography for a seed grant enabling me to undertake and transcribe interviews with new mothers in South Hampshire. And I also thank both the School of Geography at the University of Southampton and the School of Geography and Planning at Cardiff University for the space, time and resources necessary to undertake this project as a whole, especially year-on-year research funding through which I was able to receive valuable feedback on earlier versions of this work at conferences between 2008 and 2017.

I have been honoured to share earlier versions of this work as an invited speaker at Bristol University, Keele Law School, Limrick University, Queen Mary University, the University of Exeter, the University of Dundee, Brunel University and Rensselaer Polytechnic Institute, as well as at meetings of the Association of American Geographers, the Institute of British Geographers and the Royal College of Nurses. I heartily thank all those who helped facilitate these trips and especially for the valuable feedback I received at them. This commentary has helped progress my thinking on these issues immensely over the years. I particularly want to thank Nancy Campbell for her kind hosting on my trip to Rensselaer in 2014 and Anne Marie Mol for her insightful comments on work that has become chapter 3 at the Emotional Geographies Conference in Gronningen, the Netherlands. The feedback I received at these meetings was particularly useful in refining my thinking on the question of material agency in infant feeding. Thanks also go to Diana Beljaars and John Clayton for giving me the opportunity to present work from this project as a keynote talk at the 2016 'Spaces of Desire' Conference at Cardiff. I was honoured to participate in that fantastic event. John, you are missed.

The research and writing of this book were undertaken during my tenure at two universities: Southampton and Cardiff. I want to heartily thank my lovely colleagues for their camaraderie and spirit, with particular thanks going to Suzy Reimer, Emma Roe, Andy Power and Justin Spinney, with whom I was able to co-author an earlier version of what has become chapter 2. You have been both good sources of stories on the vicissitudes of early parenting and good friends. I also want to thank Linda Layne, Kim England and Wendy Larner for their myriad forms of support they have generously given over the years, and my postgraduate students Emma Waight, Carla Barrett and Eleni Bourantani. I am so proud of each of you, as well as grateful for the opportunity to learn alongside you. I thank SNP MP Alison Thewliss for the opportunity to participate in the All-Party Parliamentary Group on Infant Feeding and Inequality with whom I was able to share findings from this work. I thank Nicki Symes for welcoming me into the practitioner-focused Bristol-based Infant Nutrition and Nurture Network, and my Deleuze reading group, without whom I doubt I would ever have made it through one plateau. I would especially like to thank Aimee Grant for her careful reading and useful feedback on drafts of several chapters. And I should like to thank Great Western Railways, in whose carriages I wrote a significant portion of this text!

Over the years I have had the good fortune to have worked alongside Sally Dowling in nursing and midwifery at the University of the West of England. I have profited from this affiliation both in terms of friendship and in terms of intellectual enrichment, and especially from the Economic and Social Research Council (ESRC) networking series on breastfeeding that came out of our shared interests. I want to thank my NHS mums group in Southampton as we figured out early motherhood together, and my 'school gate' friends at Brunel Field Primary School in Bristol as we learned about not-so-early motherhood together. I am deeply grateful to the many kind care workers at Ashley Down after-school club, Art Raft Nursery in Bristol and the Trees Nursery in Southampton: you have been an indispensable part of our parenting assemblage. And I want to thank dear friends Deb Martin, Anna Skeels, Courtney Burke, Patty Billen, Becky Corso, Maia Boswell-Penc and Maria Fannin. Where would I be without your intellect, wisdom, humour, lovely food and shared glasses of wine over the years?

A special deep thanks go to my parents, Ann and Paul Boyer, and parents-in-law, Diane Maneri and Wally Buser. This book is in every way the result of your love, support and faith in me over the years. And I have saved my most important thanks for last: Michael Buser and Jake Buser Boyer. My deep thanks to both of you, for all that you have given me, including making my own experience of motherhood possible.

NOTES

1. These data sets will be described in more detail in subsequent chapters.

2. It should also be recognised that the meanings of these intersecting forms of social differentiation change over time and that within any one (intersectional) social location lies infinite forms of difference. Van der Tuin and Dolphijn refer to this as the 'thousand tiny intersections' (Van der Tuin and Dolphijn, 2012: 140) that lie beneath any identity, bringing a Deleuzian lens to the concept of intersectionality. This insight serves as an important reminder of the fact that social markers such as race, class, gender and so on can never fully capture the myriad differences within any given identity.

3. Noting also that social contexts are themselves in continual states of flux.

4. While also recognising, of course, other than hetero-normative family arrangements such as lesbian, gay and transgender and other gender-non-conforming parents.

5. At the time of writing women are entitled fifty-two weeks of maternity leave in the UK. Employed women are typically entitled thirty-nine weeks of statutory maternity pay, which is 90% of one's wage for the first six weeks and £138 a week for the remaining thirty-three weeks. The state currently offers two-week paid paternity leave (in addition to maternity leave) and up to twenty-six weeks 'additional paternity leave' if the mother or co-adopter returns to work. Additional paternity leave (APL) is remunerated at £138 a week.

6. I also recognise that this work is done by other familial and non-familial carers beyond the parent or parents (including foster parents, nursery nurses, grandparents, nannies). While the journeys of these carers are also interesting, they are beyond the scope of this work.

Chapter 1

Maternal becomings: Space, time and subjectivity in early motherhood

This chapter focuses on new mothers' emergent sense of self. Questions of subjectivity came to the fore in geography in the 1990s as scholarly engagements with feminism, queer studies, critical race studies, postcolonialism and disability studies began to flourish (Bell and Valentine, 1995; Fincher and Jacobs, 1998; Keith and Pile, 2004). Through that decade there came to be an increasing awareness of and interest in concepts of difference and otherness within the discipline. Especially with the rise of feminist geography, there came to be a growing recognition of the importance of attending to the spaces and experiences of marginalised subjects. The 1990s also marked a time of growing recognition and interest in the ways peoples' understandings of themselves emerge through spatial practice.

This scholarship highlighted the way different aspects of identity (e.g., race, class, gender and sexuality) come to have meaning through everyday spatial practice, and how power asymmetries of racism, classism, sexism, heterosexism and other forms of discrimination operate in and through space. At the same time, this scholarship also highlighted the inherent *instability* and *multiplicity* of identity 'categories' by showing how identities are made (and remade) both through one another (intersectionality) and within particular cultural, historical, biological and technological contexts (Massey, 2006). These interventions have led to a rich body of scholarship on how different kinds of identities have come to be produced under different cultural and political milieus and to a lesser extent in different historical time periods (Bell and Valentine, 1995; Fincher and Jacobs, 1998; Keith and Pile, 2004). Yet while geography scholarship has done a good job of exploring how identity gets constructed differently in different places and cultural contexts, less work has attended to how identities themselves change over time.[1]

This chapter considers early motherhood as a case of subject transformation. For many women, the experience of new motherhood can bring with it a sense of profound disorientation or deterritorialisation from one's former sense of self. In this chapter I explore trends in how new mothers in the UK understand their emergent subjectivities drawing on women's narrations of their experiences in the first year post-birth. Clearly, the relation to one's new baby is a key component to one's identity as a new mother (Baraitser, 2009), as is the formation of new relations to place and space, as I will discuss in chapter 2. In addition to the way these relations shape new mothers, in this chapter I argue that the transition to motherhood involves forming new relationships both to time itself and to one's former – and future – selves. Empirically this analysis is based on interviews with twenty mothers in London undertaken in 2011 and 2012 and an analysis of non-password-protected online discussion boards on the popular UK parenting website mumsnet between 2006 and 2014. Based on these data I argue that early motherhood can be understood as a kind of becoming.

I frame this argument through the conceptual work of Rosi Braidotti (2002) and that of Deleuze and Guattari (1983, 2004). In developing this argument I highlight the importance of time and temporality in understanding transformations to motherhood. I further argue that change over time is a highly productive (but underexplored) way of understanding subjectivity and suggest that approaching the process of subject formation as an ongoing process marks an important conceptual innovation within geography. This chapter is composed of three parts. After providing an overview of scholarship on maternal subjectivity within and beyond geography, I turn to outline my conceptual framework and empirical base. I then move on to my analysis, highlighting themes of time and the invocation of past, present and future selves undertaken by mothers in the first year post-birth as they seek to understand their new mothering selves.

EXPLORING MATERNAL SUBJECTIVITY

The question of what happens to women's identities and sense of self when they become mothers has been explored by writers, poets, artists and scholars across the arts, humanities, social sciences, healthcare sciences and medicine. Much of this scholarship has been informed by the foundational work of Adrienne Rich highlighting the fundamental tension between the power of procreation and the ways motherhood as a social practice is constrained under patriarchy (Rich, 1995) and Sara Ruddick's development of the concept of maternal practice or mothering as a verb or a kind of doing (1989).[2] Over the years, scholarship in this field has flourished with the emergence of motherhood studies as a distinct field of scholarship. This field has produced myriad insights across both academic and popular titles, and it is beyond the scope of this chapter to provide an exhaustive discussion of this literature. One of the largest areas of attention has been the pressures of striving towards aspirational/impossible goals of simultaneously being a 'devoted mother' and a 'high-achieving worker' under neoliberalism (Asher, 2011; Boyer, 2014; Hays, 1998; Warner, 2006). This body of scholarship has also addressed the role of new technologies in the journey to and experiences of parenthood (Nahman, 2013); mothers' experiences raising transgender children (Pearlman, 2010); feelings of ambivalence about motherhood (Hollway and Featherstone, 1997; Parker and Bar, 1996); and different forms of mother-activism (O'Reilly, 2010).

As noted in the introduction, this scholarship has also examined the many ways in which experiences of motherhood and mothering subjectivities emerge through multiple intersecting relations of social identity. For example, in a North American context, Vasquez (2010) has examined Chicana mothers' efforts to counter cultural messages about discrimination as part of their parenting practice, while Murphy-Geiss (2010) has analysed Muslim mothers' struggles to honour traditional Islamic values in Western contexts marked by Islamophobia. Extending analysis beyond straight families, Gabb (2005) and Taylor (2009) have explored intersecting factors of sexual orientation and class among lesbian and other non-heterosexual parents in the UK context.

As an exhaustive review of this field is beyond the scope of this chapter,[3] I will focus on how the work presented here builds on scholarship within the social sciences (and particularly geography) relating to motherhood and maternal subjectivity. Over the past twenty years a growing number of scholars in feminist geography have begun to attend to the spaces and practices of motherhood (see, e.g., England, 1996; Holloway, 1999; Katz and Monk, 1993; Longhurst, 2008; Luzia, 2010, 2013; Madge and O'Connor, 2005; McDowell et al., 2005; Mitchell et al., 2004; Pratt, 2012; Valentine, 1997). This scholarship has highlighted the fact that both experiences of motherhood and broader cultural understandings and expectations thereof vary significantly over place and time and are shaped by factors of race, class, sexual orientation and other attributes (Davidson, 2001; Holloway, 1999; Longhurst, 2000; Luzia, 2010, 2013; Madge and O'Connor, 2005; Valentine, 1997).

Scholars in feminist geography have noted how motherhood functions as a transformative experience for many women (Davidson, 2001; Madge and O'Connor, 2005) and that many new mothers and fathers find parenting overwhelming at times (Aitken, 2000). Concerning the question of identity in relation to the transition to motherhood, McDowell et al. (2005) and Holloway (1999) note the centrality of caring in most women's new identities as mothers and highlight the way normative understandings about what constitutes 'good' mothering are both shaped by the discourses of parenting 'experts' – which change over time with shifts in 'expert' opinion – and vary by class and locale. Following loosely from the work of Luce Irigary, Gregson and Rose (2000) suggest that maternal subjectivity can usefully be understood as indeterminate and ambiguous. Relatedly, Longhurst (2000) suggests that within any one mother there are multiple maternal identities, while Louise Holt (2013) has suggested the concept of interembodiment to highlight the way maternal subjectivity emerges relationally through (often) significant physical contact with one's baby. Exploring the question of maternal identity as a central concern, Luzia (2010, 2013) has explored the way maternal identities emerge in and through embodied spatial practice at different scales, exploring scales of home, neighbourhood and city through her study of lesbian mothers in suburban Australia.

In addition to terrestrial space, geographers have examined the role of online space in the formation of maternal identities. Through questionnaires and interviews with users of the UK website *babyworld*, for example, Madge and O'Connor (2005) note that online fora can provide an important source of companionship and support in the first year post-birth, providing mothers with an opportunity to express uncertainty and other feelings they might not disclose to friends offline. Arguing for an interpretation of early motherhood as a rite of passage, Madge and O'Connor suggest that online fora offer mothers an important outlet through which women can 'try on' different identities (see also Longhurst, 2000). Though highlighting that such fora cater largely to white, heterosexual, tech-savvy, middle-class mothers, these authors note the value of online interactions as a means for new mothers to move between maternal and other, more familiar identities.

In the interdisciplinary book *Making Modern Mothers* Thomson et al. make a number of observations about the emergence of maternal identity during pregnancy and early motherhood. Based on research from the UK they explore how differences between women can begin to emerge in light of discourses of the varying 'camps' of parenting practices (e.g., attachment parenting, 'free-range' parenting, 'teenage mother', 'working mother') (Thomson et al., 2011). They further note how women tend to describe their experiences of motherhood as a transition involving the curtailment of fun and the shift from pleasing one's self to pleasing another (206, 271) and identify 'selective remembering' as a strategy through which women forge coherent narratives about their mothering experiences (49). Sagely, they characterise birth as a 'temporal and emotional disruption that changes women's way of being in the world', going on to note that 'passing through the time zone from single woman to maternal subject has a seismic impact on all aspects of women's lives' (275).

In a similar vein, in *Making Sense of Motherhood: A Narrative Approach*, sociologist Tina Miller casts the transition to motherhood as – for most – a period of intermittent chaos or instability which gradually gives way to increasing levels of comfort with one's mothering self and (for some) the eventual inhabitation of the role of expert. Based on research from the UK, Miller also notes the societal pressure to be seen as a good mother and pressure to narrate one's experience of motherhood in terms of competence and the ability to cope (Miller, 2005: 62, 89). Yet amid such pressure to put on a strong face and demonstrate confidence, Miller also found evidence of women reporting a sense of not knowing who they were during early motherhood, noting further that narrations of self during this time sometimes include strategic reworkings of the past (e.g., in terms of 'readiness' for or expectations about motherhood) (Miller, 2005: 102). An overarching theme through this investigation is shock at the sheer magnitude of change motherhood brings.[4] As one participant said of her transition to motherhood, 'The change to my life . . . is complete and absolute' (Miller, 2005: 103), the arresting language conveying the magnitude of this transition for many women. This feeling was echoed in this research in the words of one participant who noted, 'Jesus Christ . . . you can't prepare for it, can you, child birth' (Laura).

Approaching motherhood from the perspective of psychoanalysis, psychotherapist and feminist theoretician Lisa Baraitser takes a somewhat different view on the period of early motherhood in her book *Maternal Encounters* (Baraitser, 2009). Through engagements with Kristiva, Lacan, Irigary and others, Baraitser seeks to explore 'what motherhood is like' (rather than what it might mean) through autoethnography and reflections from her work with clients as a practitioner. Drawing loosely on Deleuze's theorisation of desire, Baraitser argues against representations of the maternal as lack (see also Shildrick, 2010). This work highlights the importance of writing in the processes by which women grapple with their experiences as new mothers (Baraister, 2009:14), together with the importance of experiences of time in maternal becomings (74–75). Through this work Baraitser eschews conceptualising motherhood as a transformation and hazards against the notion of a coherent, singular maternal identity, emphasising instead the inherently multiple and unstable nature of maternal identities.

In this chapter I build on this diverse field of scholarship by approaching the kinds of shifts in self-understanding that can occur for women in the first year post-birth through conceptual work on becoming as advanced by Braidotti, Deleuze and Guattari. As Hannah Stark (2017) has observed, there exist broad commonalities between Deleuzian philosophy and feminist philosophy in that both seek to move beyond traditional modes of Enlightenment thought, based in binary systems. Herein I seek to explore these commonalities through an analysis of the kinds of transformations that can occur in the course of becoming a mother.

CONCEPTUAL FRAMING: LARVAL IDENTITIES AND BECOMING

An engagement with the work of Deleuze and Guattari and those engaged with this body of theory (including Braidotti, Roberts, Buchanan, Colebrook and Stark, among others) provides a useful way to approach the concept of subjectivity as a dynamic process. Together these scholars outline a conceptualisation of subjectivity as a process of *becoming*, highlighting the ways understandings of self change over time. To understand how we might think about subjectivity in a Deleuzian way, let us first consider the idea of the *larval subject* (Deleuze, 1994: 118). Larvae provide a way of conceptualising selfhood as continual transition or passing-through of states in which understandings of self both extend and retain previous ways of being. This relates to the broader concept of becoming within Deleuzoguattarian thought as a 'being in the middle' rather than a destination or fixed state.

As beings whose bodies (and bodily capacities) are in a continual state of flux, larvae also relate nicely the broader corpus of Deleuzian work in which questions of 'what a body can do' (and indeed what constitutes a 'body') are posed, with myriad examples of ways in which the concept of bodies is not limited to human bodies, and indeed human bodies are not limited by the surface of the skin. Like the larval state, pregnancy and early motherhood mark a period of radical change to the body and bodily capacities. These may include gestation, birth and breastfeeding, as well as myriad forms of bodily practice such as changing nappies, clipping nails, becoming mobile with a baby, bathing, dressing, rocking a baby to sleep (in which, of course, fathers and others can also participate). These examples all fit nicely within Hannah Stark's conceptualisation of becoming as the production of 'new ways of relating to things and new embodied sensations' (Stark, 2017: 25).

Returning to Deleuze, the larva also suggests the way subjectivity relates to waves of successive temporal practice such that 'presents' always hold within them pasts, and 'the subject, at root, is the synthesis of time' (Deleuze, 1991: 93 in Roberts, 2007: 118). Put another way, becomings are always an (evolving) amalgamation of future and past (Stark, 2017: 34) (in contrast to current calls to 'live in the moment'). This formulation suggests a sense of connection, haunting or co-presence with past selves while also suggesting that the past can serve as resource in producing subjectivity.

As Deleuzian scholars note, becomings are marked in the first instance by instability (May, 2003: 147), with the becoming subject in a continual state of reinvention (Buchanan and Colebrook, 2000: 19). As Rosi Braidotti put it, within Deleuzian philosophy the subject is characterised by 'a flux of successive becomings' (Braidotti, 2002: 70), while Hannah Stark notes that 'becoming acknowledges that things exist in a state of perpetual movement and flux, it invites us to think about processes rather than static states' (Stark, 2017: 37). Within this approach selves are also figured as (internally) *multiple*, as suggested by Guattari's observation about the 'always mixed nature of the elements that make up our subjectivity' (Guattari, 1995: 7). Figuring the subject as multiple marks a departure from (or deterritorialisation of) both traditional Western philosophy and Cartesian humanism, as well as enabling a radically open approach to subjectivity (O'Sullivan, 2006; Stark, 2017).

As subjects are figured as internally multiple within Deleuzian philosophy so are they also characterised by *relationality* (Deleuze and Guattari, 1983: 36), that is, defined through their interrelations with others. As Driscoll has put it, 'For Deleuze . . . subjectivities are temporary and mobile, produced contingently by connections and disconnections between bodies and desires rather than a foundational sense of self' (Driscoll, 2000: 76). Bringing these themes to bear on feminist theorisations of subjectivity, Rosi Braidotti merges themes of multiplicity, interrelationality and flux into what she terms 'feminist Deleuzian nomadic thinking', which is characterised by the 'commitment to re-thinking subjectivity as an intensive, multiple and discontinuous process of interrelations' (Braidotti, 2002: 69).[5] This attention to relationality has reverberated through many different fields of social science and social theory, being widely taken up within both cultural geography (Massey, 2006: 37) and scholarship on parenting such as Deborah Lupton's innovative concept of 'inter-embodiment' as a way of approaching infant subjectivity (Lupton, 2013; see also Holt, 2013).

In addition to being marked by relationality, Deleuzian becomings are fundamentally about *transition*. Yet rather than the idea of moving between two fixed points or a transition with the expectation of arrival at a final (finished) state, becoming is to do with transitoriness itself, the experience of 'being in the middle' or passing through different states (Deleuze and Guattari, 2004: 381). As Buchanan and Colebrook put it, within Deleuzian becomings what's 'real' is the transition itself, not the supposedly fixed points of 'before' and 'after' states imagined as finished (Buchanan and Colebrook, 2000: 42). In this sense the becoming subject is a continual point of departure (Deleuze and Guattari, 2004: 142). Moreover, within Deleuzian becomings such departures can be 'toward anything'; they suggest a radical openness towards the future. In this way becomings have been described as movement towards the unknown (Buchanan and Colebrook, 2000: 12; Stark, 2017: 26).

Based on this body of theory, I use a conceptualisation of subjectivity as multiple, shifting and relational, in other words defined through relations with other human and non-human entities and forces over time. I further approach maternal subjectivity as culturally situated and differentiated by race, class, age, sexual orientation and other factors. Moreover, not only do mothers' understandings of self change over time, but what it means to *be* a mother also changes over time as broader social contexts change, such that neither experiences of motherhood nor maternal subjectivity is generalisable.

In what follows I will take a first cut at engaging themes of temporality and becoming in the context of women's transitions to motherhood in the contemporary UK, arguing that this approach helps advance our understanding of how maternal subjectivities are produced. My analysis rests on two sources of data: entries to a non-password-protected bulletin board on the UK parenting website *mumsnet* and talk data produced through a collaborative project on mobility in early motherhood in London undertaken with Justin Spinney in 2011 and 2012. I will now discuss each of these databases in turn.

THE STUDY

Empirically this chapter and the next draw on two sources of data. The first of these is thirty-seven interviews with twenty mothers in three inner-city East London neighbourhoods (Hackney, Islington and Newham) undertaken in 2011–2012. These data were produced as part of a project undertaken with my colleague Justin Spinney and funded by the Royal Geographical Society and the University of East London.[6] This chapter draws on interviews with the mothers within these families. These data were then combined with an analysis of 154 posts on five threads made by new mothers to the UK parenting website *mumsnet* between March 2006 and June 2014. Post-dates and names have been removed to preserve poster's privacy, and permission has been given by *mumsnet* to reprint these posts.

As noted online bulletin boards can be an important source of information and support for new mothers (Madge and O'Connor, 2005). They are available night and day whenever a parent (with an Internet connection or smartphone) has need of information and have the potential to capture a range of non-expert views on early motherhood. As well, being anonymous may enable mothers to share more, and more honestly than they might in other settings. On the other hand, there are also some limitations to online bulletin boards as data sources which also bear noting. The most striking of these factors is that the socio-demographic profile of contributors is not known.

Although demographic information on those posting to *mumsnet* is not known, like the parenting website used by Madge and O'Connor (2005) the content of *mumsnet* is largely aimed at a heterosexual, middle-class audience. The site did not contain dedicated areas for LGBTQ mums, teen mums or mums belonging to a racial or ethnic minority which could be used to build networks or highlight information on government benefits for low-income families (e.g., family tax credits). Meanwhile the visual representations on the site tend to depict white, non-teen, able-bodied heterosexual mothers and children. All of this suggests that this resource largely caters to white, middle-class, cisgender, straight mothers. The massive chat-board covers a wide range of topics and may well include information that might be of use for LGBTQ, teen, or low-income mothers; disabled mothers; or mothers of racial, ethnic or religious minorities or other marginalised groups. However, the design of the site overall is not structured to highlight this information or help mums who share a particular kind of identity to find one another.

However, the interview data from London reflect a somewhat higher degree of diversity. At the time of the project all three London boroughs where interviews were conducted were characterised by a high degree of ethnic and socio-economic diversity and transient populations, with Newham being the most diverse and transient and Islington the least. In addition to this, our recruitment strategy was chosen specifically to enhance the socio-economic and ethnic diversity of our sample. Participants were recruited through two strategies. In the first, participants were solicited through a Facebook site of expectant (mainly white, middle-class) parents participating in (fee-based) antenatal classes offered by a large UK parenting charity. With the generous help of midwives based at hospitals in each of the study sites, we then recruited more ethnically and socio-economically diverse households through NHS-sponsored, free antenatal classes.

Through this approach we achieved a diverse, highly cosmopolitan sample in which over half our study participants were not UK-born. The final sample of twenty households was composed of eight Afro-Caribbean or Asian-descended non-British households, seven households of white-British and five households of white, non-British participants. Of the twenty households, eight were in the top-income quintile, four in the second, three in the third, two in the second and three in the lowest. Four of the households were single mothers and a child. Out of the sixteen households where there were two partners, both were heterosexual with ten married and six cohabiting. All participants were first-time parents, living in a mix of owned and rented accommodations, and were between twenty-six and thirty-eight years old.

This diversity allowed us to capture a wide range of experiences. In a few instances both parents were interviewed, but in most cases it was mothers (only) who took part in the research. Two waves of fieldwork were conducted: the first between May and July 2011, approximately three months prior to the due date of the first child, and the second between January and April 2012, approximately six to eight months after the birth of the child. Three households dropped out of the second phase of fieldwork. The approach of doing successive rounds of interviewing was selected as a means of understanding the creation of mothering subjectivities as a process that occurs over time.

Through a longitudinal research design the emergence of maternal identities could be gleaned.

Interviews were approached as a 'conversation with a purpose' (Burgess, 1988: 102). Interviews were semi-structured and focused on themes of domestic imaginaries, social networks, parenting expectations/practices/norms, materialities of parenting and access and experiences of mobility. Participants were asked to describe the places they went, people they saw and things they did in a normal week. For the majority of participants this worked well with some commenting that having to think in such a way literally gave the interview its narrative as an emerging network linking both physical and social worlds (see also Chakraborty, 2009; Wridt, 2010). Interviews, which lasted between one and two hours, were digitally recorded, transcribed and then coded and analysed. All responses have been anonymised.

It is important to note that these data speak about the experiences of motherhood in just one city: and, moreover, a city that is both larger and significantly more ethnically diverse than the rest of the UK. On the one hand, this limits the generalisability of these findings in some ways. However, because of London's role as a key immigrant destination, although the research was conducted 'in just one place', this sample is extremely international in character, with 65% of respondents hailing from nations other than the UK. As such these data arguably reflect an unusually diverse range of views on the transition to motherhood (albeit in a particularly cosmopolitan setting).

It is also to be noted that the data collected for this study have been approached with the view that knowledge is produced collaboratively between researchers and research subjects. As such, the knowledge reflected here is shaped by my biography and experiences as a mother, those of my collaborator Justin Spinney as a father, and our collective experiences as white, heterosexual, middle-class parents in different locales in the south of England (including London, Southampton and Bristol). Indeed this can be understood as a *diffractive encounter* in which our biographies not only shaped how interviews unfolded, our reactions to the data and the sense we've made of participants' narratives of their experiences but also shaped our understanding of our own parenting (Lenz-Taguchi, 2012). Building on this I have analysed these data thematically taking an inductive, theory-building approach that analyses the data both through the secondary literature and through the lens of the aforementioned social theory (Kitchin and Tate, 2000).

ANALYSIS

In the remainder of this chapter I will analyse some of the practices of early motherhood to emerge from the research described earlier as kinds of becomings. I will highlight mothers' reflections on their own becomings during early motherhood that, when taken as a whole, show something of the dynamism of subjectivity at this time. I will explore themes of fear of loss of past selves, excitement for as-yet-unknown future selves, changing experiences of time in early motherhood and the role journal-writing can play in women's experiences of becoming mothers.

Analysis of *mumsnet* postings reveals sometimes profound uncertainty about one's new identity, expressed variously as feeling unknown to one's self[7] or a sense of 'losing the me-ness of me',[8] echoing Miller's observation that many women find new motherhood to feel strange (Miller, 2005: 61). As one poster put it, 'I felt as though I had been emptied out and replaced with a mother-being',[9] which chimes with Stark's description of larval subjectivity as one in which the 'self is dissolved into the ever-changing processes that constitute it' (Stark, 2017: 19). Similarly, another commentator noted, 'Why doesn't anyone warn you of this identity issue, given it is a really fundamental thing? This is something I've been worrying about and mulling over for over a year now'.[10] This was echoed in our interviews with mothers noting how having a baby had changed their friendships and created distance in certain relationships, leading some new mothers to articulate a sense of 'grieving' the loss of certain prechild relationships. The sense of early motherhood as a kind of deterritorialisation from past selves was conveyed by one commentator through her casting of this period of life as akin to the feeling of vertigo.[11]

In a related exchange one contributor commented that she was 'hoping that as time goes by . . . I can find some happy medium between (the person I used to be) and the . . . person I seem to be becoming', in response to which another commentator queried, 'So how long does it take to adjust (to being a mother)? And how do you feel when you come to be the "new you"'? Building on this exchange a third post then added, 'I'd like to know when the "new me" kicks in too. (And) my dd (darling daughter) is almost 5'![12] These comments suggest both a sense of 'being in the middle' of a transformation as discussed earlier, as well as a (rueful) acknowledgement that the in-between feeling of motherhood is, perhaps, actually an ongoing state.

Various commentators spoke of the transition to early motherhood as a change which could be positive as well as challenging. And building on the newness (and for many, strangeness) of motherhood many comments further suggested a sense of unknowingness about the future. As one commentator noted, for example, 'It's hard to articulate, but I am actually looking forward to discovering what my identity as a mum will be',[13] suggesting the openness (on the part of some new mothers at least) to the question of who one is or will become. Like the nomadic subject, such sentiments suggest recognition of having moved away from a previous self and towards something new (but as yet unknown). They relate to the concept of becoming in their openness to the unknown that is to come and the sense of 'any possible future' ahead (Stark, 2017: 29).

One of the themes to emerge from this research was that in addition to mothering subjectivities emerging through intensive relations with one's new baby, they emerged through markedly different experiences of time, or indeed through a new relationship to time itself. This manifested through the experience of time being structured by one's baby's naps and feeds, recognising that these did not typically follow the same pattern from one day to the next. This was accompanied by a swirling-together of night and day before babies fall into more regular night-time sleep patterns in a move away from pre-baby temporal rhythms or striations. The theme of early motherhood as involving a changed experience of time or temporal deterritorialisation also emerged in interviews in terms of activities involving the baby taking longer, activities of self-care (e.g., showering and eating) being completed more quickly and a release from the strictures (but also familiar predictability) of work schedules.[14] As one study participant put it: 'Pre-pregnancy, you know . . . I did have to, you know, go from A to B and had to be at B by this time, at work. Whereas now, I mean, yeah, it doesn't matter if I'm late. I mean, there's no such thing as being late'. The new sense of time in early motherhood was narrated by some study participants as a sense of temporal plenitude, an ability to feel more present or 'in the moment', as Thomson et al. also found in their work (Thomson et al., 2011: 273). Yet for others this changed relationship to time was experienced as a loss of control over one's time and inability to accomplish tasks within a set time frame, which could cause frustration.

Related to this sense of changed temporalities, respondents also noted new forms of embodied practice. For example, participants noted walking more than they had previously, as well as becoming more aware of their local surroundings and having more time to talk to neighbours and local shopkeepers. As one respondent put it, '(It's) a bit more interesting because you see more things, because you're not in a rush . . . you know, (you) stop to chat to people and take your time'. These different chronologies suggest a change in the way new mothers relate to the world around them that stands in distinction to their engagements prebirth. Yet if some mothers felt they had more time, many also reported feeling like they had less time *for themselves* (widely referred to as 'me time'). This research shows the way some mothers use their (limited) time on their own to connect to past selves in projects of imagining possible future selves.

For example, one participant made a point of visiting the National Gallery when she had a bit of time on her own, which she described as a way of retaining an identity of 'someone who could still think about big things'. This comment signalled that although having become intimately attuned to the needs of another, this mother had not relinquished her interest in and connection to the wider world. Another participant noted that she now relished solo journeys, for which she would opt to go by bus. Not as fast as the tube, she found the bus journey calmer, and in the longer journey had enough time to do crosswords, which was a pleasure she had enjoyed prior to giving birth. In this sense 'me time' was used in part to call forth and connect to 'past selves', a tendency Miller has also noted (Miller, 2005: 104).

If for some fear of losing touch with one's 'former self' was remediated by spending time alone, for others it was spending time with other people that was desired. For example, some *mumsnet* contributors noted booking in dates with friends as a way to recall and reconnect with prebaby selves[15] and recommended the same to those posting about feelings of sadness or depression over losing their sense of self.[16] As one contributor put it, 'I think my Hubby and friends will help keep me as me'.[17] This comment both reflects the relational aspect of the Deleuzian subject-in-becoming and echoes Young's observation about the importance of the past in the work of identity-construction (Young, 2005: 129). Taken together these comments also suggest something of the way Loewen Walker posits the present as 'stretching between past and future' (Loewen Walker, 2014: 46), resulting in what she calls thick time.

'Me time' was also used to reflect on present selves through activities of journal-writing, blogging and scrapbooking. For many new mothers journaling serves as a way to manage intense or overwhelming feelings. Some used a journal to express ambivalent or negative emotions, as well as more positive and joyful ones. Various *mumsnetters* told of journaling to drafts within password-protected e-mail systems, or destroying hard copy journal entries once written as a way to open a space in which they felt able to express difficult emotions. In this way some used journaling as a way to come to grips (privately) with their process of becoming. As Deleuze has noted, 'To write is to become' (Deleuze, 1990: 29), while in relation to mothering Lisa Baraitser has described writing as 'a praxis . . . through which the personal takes place' (Baraitser, 2009: 14).[18] Referring to the work of Cixous's seminal work (1976), Hannah Stark has likewise noted the important role writing can play for mothers as a means to come to grips with very new forms of embodiment and embodied experience (Stark, 2017: 16).

As me time was used to connect to past selves and discern current ones (whether through spending time alone, being with others or journaling), it was also used as a space in which to contemplate *future* selves. Like Gillian Rose's work on family photographs, journaling was used by some as a memoir of a fleeting present and means to remember the feelings and experiences of early babyhood (and early motherhood) in the future (Rose, 2003).[19] Although time in early parenthood was sometimes experienced as slow by women interviewed for this work and those posting on *mumsnet*, many new mothers were also keenly aware of what a relatively short period of time it is when babies are small and how quickly the full measure of that experience is forgotten. This was captured by one study participant who noted wistfully that 'it's all going to be different in a few years' (Charlotte), signalling both the awareness of the 'in-betweenness' of early motherhood and – tacitly – the unknowability of future.

The chronicling of early motherhood thus served not only as a means of working out one's new identity but also as a means to connect to one's *future* self when 'it's all going to be different'. As one study participant put it:

> (My blog) is . . . like a diary because it's quite nice when I have looked back on it and there are things I have forgotten and it feels quite present, you know what I mean. It's in the moment so I am pleased we've got it so I think I will keep it up. . . . *I think it will be . . . useful for me in retrospect to look back on it.* (Chloe Kay, emphasis added)

In a similar vein, some *mumsnet* contributors wrote letters in early motherhood to their children to open when they become parents themselves.[20] This passage supports the observation made by Thomson et al. about the importance of (selective) remembering in the work of life narration (Thomson et al., 2011: 49). This kind of 'generational thinking' also suggests the highly relational aspect of selfhood as described by Deleuze and Guattari.[21] At the same time these statements suggest how mothers' recordings of their processes of becoming can serve as a resource for themselves in the future.

Through these data we can see how the practice of journaling on the part of new mothers can provide a means through which women process their experiences, ways of being in the world and (changing) understandings of self. In these writings new mothers invoke past selves and spatialities beyond the time and (often tightly bound) spaces of early motherhood in order to make sense of their current becoming subject. In connecting with past selves, such as by visiting an art museum or doing a crossword on the bus, we see the desire to establish trans-temporal and trans-spatial connections between different iterations of the self. Through diary work we see a being in the middle: the anticipation of a future self that is different from the present version (though as yet unknown), together with the recognition that the current iteration of self – the new mother – is going to fade and degrade. Journal-writing calls forth an image of a future self (or even future generations not yet born) to bear witness and serve as audience to a fleeting present, the work of the Deleuzian nomadic subject ever in the journey's midst.

CONCLUSION

This chapter has argued that a temporal perspective can both enhance our understanding of early motherhood and advance conceptual work on subjectivity in geography and beyond. In the data presented here we can see early motherhood as a kind of becoming. I have shown different ways in which maternal subjects can be viewed as a 'synthesis of time' (Deleuze, 1991: 93 in Roberts, 2007: 118), and some of the ways past selves continue to reverberate within current understandings of self for new mothers. I have further suggested that early motherhood is a kind of movement both through and towards the unknown, an experience of 'being in the middle' or transition without expectation of eventual arrival at some fixed, finished future state.

This process is relational, produced through interactions not only with babies, partners, friends and family but also with past and future selves. I have argued here, in early motherhood we can see Braidotti's feminist Deleuzian subject: unstable, multiple, relational and characterised by a 'flux of successive becomings' (Braidotti, 2002: 70). I have shown how new mothers are simultaneously 'in the moment', aware of both how different their lives are from what they have been and how much they will continue to change moving onwards. In this sense, new motherhood is perhaps more than anything a time in which change itself becomes the norm: it is marked by the production of new relationships with time itself. Having explored new mothers' changing relationships with time, chapter 2 considers their changed relationships with space through an analysis of journey-making and changed experiences of public space for new mothers.

NOTES

1. Although this is beginning to change. See, for example, Madge and O'Connor (2005) and work in disability studies for important contributions in this area.

2. Defining motherhood as a practice 'as a verb' or doing is how some scholars have advanced the idea of male mothers.

3. See the introduction of Andrea O'Reilly's *Twenty-First Century Motherhood* for a good overview of this field.

4. As others also note the transition to motherhood can also be associated with identity crisis (Figes, 1998).

5. Nomadism is cast by Deleuze and Guattari as a continual becoming.

6. These data were collected by Spinney and analysed by Boyer and Spinney.

7. http://www.mumsnet.com/Talk/parenting/a159906-have-you-lost-your-identity.

8. http://www.mumsnet.com/Talk/pregnancy/2113216-feel-like-Ive-already-lost-my-identity-feeling-down.

9. http://www.mumsnet.com/Talk/parenting/a159906-have-you-lost-your-identity.

10. http://www.mumsnet.com/Talk/parenting/a159906-have-you-lost-your-identity.

11. http://www.mumsnet.com/Talk/pregnancy/2113216-feel-like-Ive-already-lost-my-identity-feeling-down.

12. Comments from http://www.mumsnet.com/Talk/parenting/a159906-have-you-lost-your-identity.

13. http://www.mumsnet.com/Talk/pregnancy/2113216-feel-like-Ive-already-lost-my-identity-feeling-down. Interestingly another commentator noted that she felt 'more like herself' than before birth.

14. This relates to Karen Davies's (1990) framework of contrasting approaches to time associated with wage-work as being discontinuous as opposed to caregiving as being continuous and responsive to the needs of others. See Baraitser (2008) for a different view on 'maternal time' as being fundamentally based on disruption.

15. http://www.mumsnet.com/Talk/pregnancy/2113216-feel-like-Ive-already-lost-my-identity-feeling-down.

16. http://www.mumsnet.com/Talk/parenting/a159906-have-you-lost-your-identity.

17. http://www.mumsnet.com/Talk/pregnancy/2113216-feel-like-Ive-already-lost-my-identity-feeling-down.

18. See also Juhausz (2003).

19. See also http://www.mumsnet.com/Talk/parenting/a331859-anyone-else-keep-a-kind-of-journal-diary-of-their.

20. http://www.mumsnet.com/Talk/parenting/a331859-anyone-else-keep-a-kind-of-journal-diary-of-their.

21. This also chimes with the work of Thomson et al. (2011) in which they observed that 'through accommodating highly charged feelings within the seemingly banal activities that give shape to the everyday, (new mothers are) active in the accomplished project of transition, a state that moves towards forms of settlement between past and present while anticipating new deals between the present and the future' (2011: 274).

Chapter 2

Mothering with the world: Spatial practice, mobility and material agency in maternal becomings[1]

As discussed in the previous chapter, the transition to motherhood typically marks a profound change to one's sense of self and ways of engaging with the world (Bailey, 1999; Miller, 2005). For many, the experience of new motherhood is a shockingly affecting one, described by *Guardian* writer Stephen Voss as 'the blast zone' (Voss, 2017: 18).[2] This chapter is about some of the practices that constitute the shock of new motherhood, focusing on the entanglements or mutually affecting engagements with the more-than-human (including matter, affects and policies) that occur in the course of trying to become mobile with a small baby. Drawing on interviews with new mothers in East London, I analyse the relationships between discourses of parenting and the material practices of journey-making. Contributing to conceptual work on the New Materialism (Alaimo and Hekman, 2008; Braidotti, 2002; Coole and Frost, 2010) and mobility studies (Cresswell, 2010; Urry, 2000; Ziegler and Schwanen, 2011), I advance the concept of mother–baby assemblages as a way to understand mobile motherhood, and consider the emotional and affective dimensions of parenting in public that emerge through journey-making.

Through an analysis of engagements with the material world that occur in the course of journey-making for new mothers, I seek to deepen both our understanding of mobility as a relational practice and our understanding of the spatial politics of early motherhood. This chapter advances scholarship by highlighting the utility of conceptual work from the New Materialism as a means of better appreciating the role of relations with the non-human in theorising social experience. I suggest that the focus on human–non-human entanglements within the New Materialism advances scholarship in and beyond geography by enabling conceptualisations of action, space and social life which are richer and more complete.

This chapter builds on scholarship on the politics of im/mobility (Cresswell, 2010) and responds to calls to apply a mobilities perspective to the study of families (Holdsworth, 2013). Analysis rests on a robust empirical base of thirty-seven interviews with twenty new mothers in two ethnically and socio-economically diverse neighbourhoods in East London, focusing on experiences of mobility after the birth of a first child.[3] Responding to Cresswell's provocation to attend to the affective dimensions of journey-making (Cresswell, 2010), there has been a trend in recent geography scholarship to focus on mobility's joyful, liberating and well-being-producing aspects (Latham and McCormack, 2004; Milligan, 2003; Ronander, 2010; Ziegler and Schwanen, 2011). In contrast, the journeys encountered in the course of this research were more often marked by slowness, discomfort, premeditation and feelings of exhaustion (if not dread), thus building on the conceptual work of Adey (2006), Bissell (2009), Holdsworth (2013) and Hubbard and Lilley (2004). Given that most people become parents at some point in their lives,[4] I suggest that these more arduous forms of mobility warrant our critical attention.

This chapter is divided into four parts. After tracing out the conceptual lenses I use to develop my analysis in this chapter (building on the conceptual work outlined in chapter 1), I then turn to explore the concept of mother–baby assemblages. I then explore what happens when mother–baby assemblages become mobile and finally analyse the transpersonal intensities that emerge from mothering in public in the course of journey-making.

CONCEPTUAL FRAMEWORK

Building on the conceptual frame outlined in the introduction and developed in chapter 1 in relation to the concept of becoming, this chapter draws on theoretical work from the intersecting fields of the New Materialism (Coole and Frost, 2010), feminist materialism (Alaimo and Hekman, 2008; Braidotti, 2002) and assemblage theory (Deleuze and Guattari, 1983, 2004) to analyse the linkages between materiality and mobility as an embodied experience. As noted in chapter 1, I am particularly interested in how these bodies of work forefront relationality and help bring discourse-based ways of understanding the world into communication with more materially and affectively based ways.

Influenced by the work of Deleuze and Guattari, the New Materialism and feminist materialism approach both matter and embodied subjects as simultaneously engaged in ongoing processes of transformation while at the same time being situated within extant categories of social, biological, technological and other forms of classification that can be very slow to change.

As noted, the New Materialism seeks to decentre the human subject as the sole or primary ontological concern, instead widening the aperture to focus on the different ways that living and nonliving matter interrelate and affect one another. Working across fields of philosophy, political theory and women's studies, this body of scholarship is concerned with the forms of relationality which develop between matter, discourse, affect and politics in a way that 'insist(s) upon the meaning, force, and value of materiality' (Alaimo and Hekman, 2008: 10). In light of this work, I recognise subjects as being in a state of constant (though sometimes gradual) change, as both cultural contexts and bodily compositions shift over time.

Concepts from the New Materialism have begun to circulate within geography over the past ten years (Braun, 2015; Latham and McCormack, 2004; Lorimer, 2008; Simpson, 2013; Whatmore, 2006). Fuelled by a broader interest in the Anthropocene, this work has sought to explore the agentic properties of matter and the more-than-human especially through scholarship on naturecultures (Braun, 2015; Lorimer, 2008; Whatmore, 2006) and the ways urban form acts upon the wider urban environments of which it is a constitutive part (Latham and McCormack 2004; Simpson, 2013). I am excited by what these interventions reveal about the importance of non-human actants in shaping our world and for helping bring forth more expansive and less human-centric understandings of agency. At the same time, I suggest that this body of philosophy holds utility beyond what has currently been explored. In addition to the ways the New Materialism has been engaged to date, this body of theory constitutes a fruitful and as-yet underutilised resource as a means of conceptualising socio-spatial relations.

In her book *Maternal Encounters* social psychologist Lisa Baraitser has called for attending to 'the mutually constitutive relationships between the human and non-human' that occur in the course of parenting (Baraitser, 2009: 138). Within geography, explorations of the role of the more-than-human in the course of parenting have included exploring how mothers' identities are formed through engagements with online support groups (as noted in chapter 1) (Madge and O'Connor, 2005); Waitt and Harada's discussion of the family car as a space in which parenting happens (Waitt and Harada, 2016); and the way baby clothes and things move through parenting assemblages (Waight, 2014).

I extend existing work within and beyond geography by considering motherhood as a practice that happens collaboratively through engagements 'with the world' (including built form, prams, slings, other people, weather, transport infrastructure) in the course of becoming mobile with a small baby. This chapter builds directly on Baraiter's work, in which she examines experiences of early motherhood in terms of alterity, interruption, transformation, love and encumbrance based on personal experience anecdotally recounted

(Baraitser, 2009: 11). Herein I extend this work by considering the affective and emotional dimensions of 'mothering in public' in the course of journey-making, exploring how early motherhood happens through engagements with the non-human in the course of becoming mobile with a small baby.

In the previous chapter I posited the transition to motherhood as a kind of metamorphosis, a stage in an ongoing process of becoming. Building on this, in this chapter I argue that this shift occurs in part through relations with the material world, on the one hand, and discourses about (good and bad) parenting, on the other. Following Karan Barad I approach social action as produced through engagements (or intra-actions) with material and social worlds in which neither subjects nor the environments they encounter are ontologically prior (Barad, 2008) as well as through – in this case – power-fully affective engagements with one particular being – one's new baby. After Braidotti, I understand motherhood as a case of 'the actualization of the immanent encounter between subjects, entities, and forces which are apt mutually to affect and exchange parts of each other' (Braidotti, 2002: 68), in other words, as the result of continuous comings-together of humans, non-humans and other forces. As noted, I approach the 'mothering subject' as shifting, relational and multiple and understand the practice of mothering as highly variable across time, space and culture, as well as by factors of socio-economic class, race, ethnicity, sexual orientation and other factors. However, moving outwards from 'mothers themselves' as was the focus of chapter 1, in this chapter and the next I balance my concern with mothers and babies with an equal concern for different forms of more-than-human agencies.

In my exploration of the relational dimensions of mothering in this chapter I draw on both the concept of transpersonal intensities (Anderson, 2009), which I take to mean the work emotions do in connecting people and creating a certain mood or feeling in a space, and that of assemblage, in the sense of different things or parts joining together to do something (Gill-Peterson, 2013). Drawing on the work of Deleuze and Barad, I employ the concept of assemblages as a means of attending to the 'ongoing flow of agency through which "part" of the world makes itself . . . intelligible to another "part" of the world' (Barad, 2008: 135). After Deleuze and Guattari I invoke this concept as a way to speak about how things (or more typically parts of things) come together in a 'machenic relation' to one another, or, as Hannah Stark puts it, a relation in which one's body finds a new function (Stark, 2017: 25). Deleuze and Guattari illustrate the concept of the assemblage through various examples, including how wasps and orchids work together to achieve plant pollination (Deleuze and Guattari, 2004: 293); how breasts and babies work together to achieve breastfeeding (Deleuze and Guattari, 1983: 50–51 in Hickey-Moody, 2013: 274–275); or how horses and riders work together to achieve warriors (Deleuze and Guattari, 2004: 440).

I suggest that assemblages provide a useful way to put the New Material-ism's call to decentre the human subject into practice, by shifting focus to the role the constituent parts of a given assemblage play in completing a task. I further propose that the assemblage provides a useful way to conceptualise early motherhood. In this chapter I employ the concept of the assemblage to show how mothers come together with babies, prams/slings, public transport systems, policies and publics to achieve mobility, exploring some of the diffuse agencies at play in those processes. Employing a new materialist approach, I focus on the entanglements which connect bodies and artefacts within such assemblages (or in Karen Barad's parlance, 'phenomena'), with the understanding that the practices connecting bodies and artefacts play a central role in creating the meanings these 'things' come to have.

In addition to advancing understanding about the spaces and politics of motherhood through an engagement with the New Materialism and assem-blage theory, I seek to make an intervention in the mobilities literature. In line with Cresswell (2010) another goal of this chapter is to develop an under-standing of mobility that can inform theorisations of gendered social identi-ties such as motherhood. I argue that mobility is an important dimension through which women come to know themselves as mothers. It is through being mobile that mothers learn how to use particular objects to hone their parenting skills; introduce their children to new experiences, test out their emerging and evolving identities and come to know their new 'parented' body. As Cresswell states, 'Getting from A to B can be very different depend-ing on how the body moves. Any consideration of mobility has to include the kinds of things people do when they move in various ways' (Cresswell, 2010: 20). I seek to highlight how the materiality associated with travel 'pushes back' on new mothers to shape experiences of mobility. In line with the mobilities turn, I theorise mothers' (often limited and fraught) mobility as produced through the coming together of bodies, competencies, objects and landscapes, thus highlighting the highly relational nature of mobility.

Regarding transport geography, Cresswell argues that researchers 'have developed ways of telling us about the fact of movement, how often it happens, at what speeds, and where. Recently, they have also informed us about who moves and how identity might make a difference' (2010: 19). Such accounts position movement as an outcome rather than a process or accomplishment. They tell us little about how forms of mobility coalesce or disintegrate. Cresswell also notes that at any given historical moment there are constellations of movement, meaning and practice that make sense together (2010: 18). I suggest that this is not quite accurate in that these con-stellations do not just make sense, rather they are made sense of: an accom-plishment that requires no small amount of labour. Indeed the character and ultimately tendency towards mobility or immobility are shaped through the doing of parenting in particular circumstances with particular equipment and competencies.

A final point I wish to make in this chapter is that mobility is a key area in which family is enacted (even if the actual experiences of journey-making for new mothers are often less than ideal). As Holdsworth (2013) has pointed out, there appears to be a dominant assumption that the excessive mobility of the modern Western family is 'anti-family'. The assumption seems to be that families should be largely immobile, with short commutes to work and school and an extended family close at hand. This geographical imaginary of family harks back to a Heideggerian and sedentarist notion that attachment is something that occurs (only) when dwelling in place, rather than on the move (Cresswell, 2006; Urry, 2000: 133).

Clearly, distance can constitute very real barriers for parents, as Gerry Pratt's work on Filipina women employed as nannies in Canada while parenting their own children at great distance has amply shown (Pratt, 2012). But as the mobilities scholarship has shown, attachment can also take place both in and through mobility (Cresswell, 2006; Holdsworth, 2013; Spinney, 2006, 2010). Holdsworth in particular has explored ways families find to 'construct connectedness' despite geographical distances (2013: 3). Though focusing primarily on well-resourced families in the Global North, she notes that for such families distance 'does not necessarily reduce the social and emotional significance of bonds between people' (Holdsworth, 2013: 4). Building on this, in this chapter I seek to extend understanding about how 'bonds between people are created, transformed and retained through movement and mobility' (ibid.). In this chapter I illustrate the ways mobility and immobility can be both complementary and antagonistic to the construction of parental identities and understandings of family.

THE STUDY

Like chapter 1 this chapter is based on thirty-seven interviews with twenty families in three inner-city East London neighbourhoods (Hackney, Islington and Newham) collected in 2011 and 2012.[5] As noted in the previous chapter this data set reflects social diversity in a number of respects. The sample of twenty households included eight Afro-Caribbean or Asian descended non-British families, five white non-British families and seven white-British families. Three of the families were in the lowest economic quintile and two more were in the second-lowest. Though as a group this sample was still more economically privileged than the UK as a whole, this degree of diversity allows at least a glimpse of parenting experiences across a range of socio-economic backgrounds. It also enables a view into a wide range of different kinds of mobilities, with some participants taking frequent and/or very distant journeys, and others taking relatively few, as well as engagement with a range of different modes of travel (including walking, bus, train, tube, bicycle, car and air).[6]

At the same time it should be noted that these data speak to experiences of parental mobility in just one city and, moreover, a city that has both unusually extensive systems of public transportation and in which car ownership is very expensive and on the decline.[7] While this limits the generalisability of this work in some ways, given that most existing literature on parenting focuses on either suburban or car-based forms of journey-making (Dowling, 2000; Luzia, 2010), a consideration of less auto-dependent forms of parental mobilities both fills an empirical gap and fulfils an important political objective of highlighting more sustainable forms of mobility. As well, this sample is highly international in character, with 65% of our respondents being immigrants. As such I suggest that these data reflect a significant range of views regarding parenting, journey-making and mobility.

MOTHERS AND BABIES ASSEMBLED

All the stuff you have with babies . . . the amount of stuff is shocking.
(Laura, study participant, 2011)

Prams and/or slings, nappies, wipes, muslins, pacifiers, onesies/vests. Bottles, breast pump(s), formula. Teething gel, nappy rash-cream, baby shoes-socks-hats-mittens. Toys! Snacks, play mats. Tiny blankets, mattresses, fitted sheets, teddies, mobiles, night lights. For most non-poor denizens of advanced capitalist countries, the transition to parenthood involves becoming awash in a significantly new material landscape. As Lisa Baraitser puts it, 'Where there is a mother and infant there is always some stuff' (Baraitser, 2009: 125). As the consumption literature has argued, decisions about what to buy for one's baby are bound up with the production of maternal identities (Clarke, 2004) while the act of provisioning for a baby has been described as an expression of love in itself (Miller, 1998). I seek to build on analyses which focus on shopping to think on how particular objects become interwoven with parenting practice in the context of daily use. My guiding questions are what are the relations between the different bodies and materials that mothers assemble in order to make journeys; how and why do certain assemblages stabilise (and destabilise); what are the relations between these assemblages and discourses of parenting; and how do encounters with the material world feed into first-time mothers' (evolving) understandings of themselves?

Prams[8] (also called baby carriages or buggies) can be understood as a 'kinship object' (Carsten, 2004) of early motherhood in the UK (and many other places) both for how they suggest a particular kind of kin relationship and for their standing as an almost definitional artefact to the practice of early motherhood.[9] As Baraitser argues (drawing on Serres, 1995), matter and objects (such as prams) function to stabilise human relationships (Baraitser, 2009: 137). Following a science and technology studies (STS) approach (Layne et al., 2010), prams can be seen to reflect and reproduce such values as the benefit of fresh air for babies and the benefit of walking as a mode of transport. They anticipate an able-bodied pram-pusher and destinations (including kin and friendship networks) within walking distance (whether or not this is the case).

For the moment, however, I would like to bracket a longer discussion of the politics of pram design in order to consider some of the different ways that prams, babies and mothers come together to create assemblages. Parenting assemblages form between a wide range of human and non-human entities from grandparents, other parents, health visitors and paediatricians to night lights, teddies, baby ibuprofen and so forth. Due to space limitations I focus here on what is arguably the key element of mobile mother–baby assemblages, the pram or baby buggy, and attend to the different kinds of agencies and forces that mother–baby–pram assemblages activate.

The profusion of stuff that can go along with early parenting makes a problem for many mothers and fathers in terms of mobility. Prams partially solve these problems, providing a means to carry not only a baby (or babies) but also a selection of baby-detritus which might be brought along on a given journey (pacifier, nappies, wipes, change mat, sun hat, rain gear, change of clothes, bottle, small toys, snacks). Prams relate to discourses about parenting by enabling mothers and fathers to 'be prepared', by bringing along materials for a range of different eventualities. For example, as one participant noted of the contents of her pram, 'there's a lot of "in-case" stuff in there' (Clara), hinting at the way prams can help satisfy new mothers' desire to appear competent to themselves and others (Miller, 2005: 62). Prams remain the normative way of getting around with a baby in the UK and prospective parents such as Mary were told by close relatives that without a pram 'you'll find it very difficult' (Mary).

While the mothers in this study appreciated the ability to carry baby-gear (in addition to their baby) that prams afforded, they also expressed ambivalence about the kinds of assemblages that resulted. As one participant noted, 'Whenever I go out with the pram I do feel a bit like I'm twice the size, and I'm a lot more aware of how annoying that must be for people' (Clara). Or, as another respondent put it:

> It's like when you go backpacking and you have a big bag, and you end up filling it no matter what size it is. . . . I've got all kinds of crap in there. So yeah,

that's another reason I don't really like taking the pushchair, because I feel like I'm a bag lady, well, like Bubbles in 'The Wire', you know. He's got these trolleys just full of random stuff. (Mary)

These passages suggest some of the anxieties about what prams 'do' to mothers' bodies, in terms of extending them in ways many participants did not like (or worried others did not like). This resonates with the work of Baraitser, who has noted that mothers are

> often weighed down by a number of other objects she brings with her so that her hands are not free, so that her body is not mobile in the same way as it used to be. She is encumbered, not just by the physical presence of a child who needs holding, carrying, who walks at a quarter of her speed, who pulls on her legs, but by the multiplicity of relationships negotiated with child, environment and stuff. (Baraitser, 2009: 130)

For some participants, the bigness and unwieldiness of their 'prammed' bodies coupled with the multitude of new relationships with the world that needed negotiating in the course of becoming mobile created a mother–baby assemblage that was felt to be cumbersome to the point of being ridiculous.

In addition to anxiety about the way prams extend the parenting-body study participants expressed awareness (and often unease) about the ways prams positioned them in relation to others. As one respondent put it, 'I didn't want to be there with the sort of buggy and "sorry I am a mum", you know what I mean' (Emma), signalling concern about mother–baby assemblages being perceived as a nuisance. To others, such assemblages not only marked maternal identity but also threatened to subsume 'other-than-parent' aspects of the self. As one participant put it, 'If you go around with a buggy you are a mum: no one sees you as you' (Rosa). I suggest that comments such as these highlight the co-constitutive nature of human–non-human relations that can develop in early motherhood. In the swirling together of 'mum' and 'pram', this respondent suggests how her identity as a mum became fixed by her (physical) relation to the pram, by 'going around with it'.

Prams also came up in discussions with study participants as a way of mediating a baby's behaviour and especially as a means to induce sleep, which was noted as both good for the child as well as giving the mother a moment to relax. Consider the following: 'You know that you can push her somewhere, then you might go to the café, and . . . instead of having to sit there with a baby sleeping on you, she can sleep over there, and you can have a coffee' (Mary). Here, the prams' ability to 'take the baby off you', to enable a short break from the physical and emotional demands of caring for a young baby was noted and appreciated, echoing the point that David Bissell has made that for encumbered urban subjects 'relaxation . . . is the invitation to momentarily relinquish (their) prostheses' (Bissell, 2009: 182). This respondent went on to comment, 'She must feel comfortable in there, because sometimes if she's feeling grumpy, if I just put her in there she'll just go to sleep, which is amazing, because she never does that in her cot, or anywhere else' (Mary). Together these comments suggest some of the ways participants used prams strategically to mediate their baby's mood and somatic state (in the case of babies who sleep well in prams), sometimes finding in them unexpected affordances.

For others, however, dissatisfaction with prams led those assemblages to destabilise, and these mothers often used a sling either alongside or instead of a pram.[10] Some participants appreciated how slings could ease the burden of travelling on busses and trains, or allow them to extend the capacity of their mother–baby assemblage. For example, while some babies slept beautifully in their prams, others would only sleep in a sling (or equivalent), leading to journeys in which a baby spent some of the time awake in a pram, and the rest asleep in a sling (with bags of grocery shopping often taking the baby's place in the pram).[11] Some participants also preferred having their babies closer to their own bodies, especially in the context of a dense urban environment and when crossing busy roads. Others cast slings as a more familiar-seeming form of mobility after the experience of pregnancy. As one respondent noted, 'Having her in the sling was basically just like she was still inside me', going on to add that 'I was very used to being pregnant. . . . I wasn't used to having a vehicle with me the whole time' (Emma). This comment highlights how some mothers were drawn to slings as a means of recreating a bodily relation with one's baby that recalled pregnancy.

And for some participants, slings appealed as a means of simply reducing the complexity of their mother–baby assemblage. These mothers challenged the received list of things they 'must' bring with them and ways they should relate to the detritus of early parenting (and by extension, also parental discourses about the importance of 'being prepared'). As one participant put it, 'I kind of just think, "well, you know what, if I really need something, I'll work it out when I get there. I'll borrow something, I'll make something' (Clara). I would make three observations about this comment. First, it suggests both the sheer enormity of the physical task of becoming mobile with a baby (by whatever means), as well as the desire of some new mothers to travel lighter, to scale back their engagements with the 'things and stuff' of parenting.[12] At the same time it also suggests the role that engagements with the material world can play in decisions about 'what kind of mother' someone will be. For some, parental competency is achieved not by bringing along lots of stuff but instead through a mixture of do it yourself (DIY) craftiness and making do with less.

This section has examined the reasons why certain mother–baby assemblages stabilise (and destabilise). I have shown how these assemblages can create sometimes unexpected affordances, how material practice and parenting discourses can be woven together and something of the role that engagements or entanglements with the material world play in the spatial practices of new mothers. The next two sections consider what happens when mother–baby assemblages become mobile.

MOTHER–BABY ASSEMBLAGES AND THE MATERIALITY OF URBAN ENVIRONMENTS

A body is achieved, not by regarding what it is, but by understanding the movements or problems that animate it. (Colebrook, 2008: 54–55)

This section and the next explore the relations between mother–baby assemblages and the environments they both produce and are produced by, drawing on Spinney's notion of 'embodied cultures of mobility' (Spinney, 2006: 713). Recalling Barad, I figure these encounters as mutually constitutive intra-actions in which neither part is ontologically prior. Building on my argument thus far that maternal subjectivities emerge out of encounters with parental 'kinship objects' such as prams, in this section I argue that mother–baby relations – and the assemblages they form – are structured through their intra-actions with the material contexts of build form. Let us begin by considering how particular kinds of material contexts structure the way mothers and babies relate to their prams. Prams figured in discussions with study participants about parenting mobilities as both an enabling and disabling force with weight, width and design (especially 'fold-ability'), all noted as important elements in decisions about how, where and how much to travel. Although the consumption literature has focused on the role of prams as status symbol (Clarke, 2004; Miller, 2005), participants in this study spent a lot of time talking about the problems with their prams.

Given London's high rates of ridership on public transportation (and relatively low rates of car ownership), experiences of public transport were a particular focus of this study. These experiences were often negative. Especially trying were two-pram limits on busses (which sometimes necessitated waiting for several busses in a row until one had space); fears about pram wheels getting stuck between train carriages and the platform; and of course stairs, which nearly every participant discussed as a problem. As one participant said of her parenting journeys, 'Yeah, what an absolute nightmare. All the trains over ground are all steps, loads and loads of steps, masses of steps, and I've been carrying the pram up and down these steps like tons of times' (Laura). Along similar lines, another participant outlined the difficulties of mobilising her mother–baby assemblage for longer, multimodal journeys thus:

> Getting on and off the train is a total nightmare . . . (the pram) doesn't collapse that easily so if I have to put it down that's quite difficult when you have to hold a baby. What I have done before is that I have got a taxi from here with the car seat, but then you still have to carry everything at the station and I am trying to save money so the bus will be better. So you have to think about the logistics and even just getting out on the day I will have to go and sort the buggy out with the car seat with her and then come back up and take all the luggage down and yeah it's a pain to be honest. (Mia)

For some, the ways prams intra-act with the rest of the urban environment led participants to organise their journeys in particular ways, such as by favouring tube stations with lifts or shops with doors wide enough to accommodate prams. Prams could also encourage new mobility patterns, such as for one participant who started frequenting a certain pub 'because it's a good place to go with the pram' (Clara).[13]

As feminist geographers and planners have noted, most cities do no cater for children or their carers (Domosh and Seager, 2001; Walker and Cavanagh, 1999; Weisman, 1994). Neither babies (nor their carers) fit within the logics of Capitalism that are largely responsible for shaping built form (e.g., speed and efficiency). As a consequence, the needs of both babies and their carers are often ignored in the public realm, as Gibson-Graham has noted (Gibson-Graham, 2006). The limited space for prams on busses and lack of lifts/elevators in tube and train stations illustrate how urban form is stratified for particular kinds of bodies and material-corporeal engagements, favouring those with the most immediate link to wage labour and disadvantaging others. Stairs, narrow doorways and the like become boundaries as they intra-act with prams. The problems and limits they place on mothers' mobility reveal 'the constitutive force of matter and materiality in the social and cultural sphere' (Lenz-Taguchi, 2012: 270). Such encounters highlight the extent to which built form anticipates bodies that are not only able-bodied (Imrie and Kumar, 1998) but also individuated and 'unencumbered'.[14]

Building on this, I argue that the forms of mediation between mother–baby assemblages and the material environments of which they are a part – such as masses of steps – mean that such assemblages do not elide with majoritarian forms of spatial practice. They do not move easily through space that is striated for production, and this is felt through bodily experience (Colebrook, 2008; Lenz-Taguchi, 2012).

Because of this, for many parents, a set of spatial practices which for others are 'in the background' – the largely routinised work of journey-making – are instead a matter of considerable thought and planning. Indeed, as in Bissell's work on prostheticised passengers (Bissell, 2009), some study participants reported feeling an affinity between themselves and people with physical disabilities, in that both constitute a departure from normative or molar forms of urban embodiment. For some this sense was intensified by additional challenges to mobility from caesarean sections or other bodily changes from giving birth or pain (e.g., bad backs, bad shoulders, 'dodgy knees') from baby-carrying, pram-hauling and/or sling-wearing.

Drawing on Latour's work on object-oriented ontology (e.g., posting the non-human as the central object of analysis), Lisa Baraitser takes attending to the more-than-human even farther, suggesting we approach mothers and babies as appendages of the pram. Building on this framework she astutely observes that 'the pram acts in all sorts of ways to both aid and fail to aid the mother in her work caring for the child', going on to note that 'in doing so it changes the relations between mother and child as well as between the mother and her environment, and ultimately the mother and herself' (Baraitser, 2009: 139).

These observations resonate with comments made by participants in this study, for whom the difficulties encountered in going out led many mothers to simply spend more time at home. As one participant put it, 'Sometimes I do think "oh, it would be nice to go to Hampstead Heath or da, da, da, or do this . . .", and I just think, God, I've not got the energy to just deal with a journey [laughter]. . . . I just think it's too tiring' (Laura). One participant confided that she 'can't bear to go down to Tesco with the buggy' (Emma), while another likened getting out the door to a military operation (Esta). This view was echoed in the sentiment: 'I guess it's why, like a lot of my friends here don't really go out . . . much, because it's just a big production' (Mary). For some, intra-actions between parent–baby assemblages and the built environment led to patterns of immobility, with trips outside the home reduced.

Yet of course, not all the mothers in this study responded to difficulties negotiating the built environment in the same way. While some reacted by limiting travel, others either took such challenges in their stride or simply claimed the space they needed to get around. For example, as one respondent said of her experiences negotiating London's many tube stations without lifts: 'I just do it, if no one is there to help I just drag the pram up. . . . It don't bother me' (Rachael). This resonates with Baraitser's likening of the way mothers with prams move through the city to parkour, in the sense that both forms of mobility involve moving around the city in a way it wasn't designed for in terms of the negotiation of myriad obstacles (Baraitser, 2009: 146–150).[15]

Similarly, study participant Emma shared that prior to having a child she had 'noticed women with big buggies just marching down the road and people are just expected to scatter . . . and now I realise you have got to do that when you are taking a buggy around with you because nobody else gets out of the way for you otherwise, and you are constantly going "sorry, sorry"'. I suggest that these practices can be read as a form of resistance to normative or majoritarian ways of engaging with the built environment (a mother dragging a pram upstairs by herself), as well as social mores around how embodied 'rights' to urban space are played out on the ground (mums 'marching' through the city).[16]

This section has focused on the ways that spaces of public transport are stratified for certain kinds of bodies and corporeo-material engagements, and how these largely exclude mothers and babies. I have suggested that it is in part through encounters with the materiality of built form (e.g., stairs and too-narrow doors) in the course of trying to become mobile with their babies that women come to know themselves as mothers (whether by shaping one's practice to avoid such barriers or in triumphing over them). Having considered what happens when mother–baby assemblages intra-act with the physical environment from the perspective of spatial practice, let us now turn to consider the emotional and affective aspects of these encounters.

JOURNEY-MAKING, MOTHERING IN PUBLIC AND TRANSPERSONAL INTENSITIES

If she's going to start crying I'm going to start panicking. (Tamanna)

The last section of this chapter explores experiences of mothering in public in the course of journey-making, focusing on the ways that bodies and non-human actants affect and are affected by one another. With Anderson (2009), Duff (2010), Stewart (2011), Buser et al. (2013) and others, I support the notion that the emotional resonances or transpersonal 'intensities' which form between bodies in a given space are a fundamental dimension of everyday experiences. In line with this literature and building on the analysis thus far, I take a new materialist approach to the production of affective environments, reading off Anderson who notes that 'affective qualities emanate from the assembling of the human bodies, discursive bodies, non-human bodies, and all the other bodies that make up everyday situations' (Anderson, 2009: 80). For this last section I turn to consider the emotions and transpersonal intensities that can emerge through the coming-together of mothers, babies, other passengers and the material environment within spaces of public transport. Anderson casts affective atmospheres as 'a class of experience that occur *before* and *alongside* the formation of subjectivity' (Anderson, 2009: 78). In this spirit, I explore the role of such experiences in the processes by which new mothers come to understand themselves as such.

Journeying on public transit is to travel alongside strangers, often in tight, enclosed spaces. Such experiences can elicit feelings of fear, anxiety, foreboding and sometimes pleasure. As noted, experiences of public transport are mediated by the built form of the transit system (the size and configuration of the seating, the size and placement of windows, stairs in stations and inside double-decker busses, the presence or absence of grab-bars, etc.); the mood, hunger and energy levels of both babies and their carers as well as time of day, train scheduling, temperature and lighting within busses and train carriages. The rest of this section considers some of the transpersonal intensities travelling with young babies can generate. I consider three kinds of events: the screaming baby, the scenario of a baby vomiting on a train and babies engaging with strangers. I suggest that travelling with babies can be experienced as a space of judgement while sometimes creating openings to remake understandings about public space.

A common theme in narrations of travelling with babies is the feeling of anxiety, epitomised by the spectre of a screaming child in a confined space. This event or, after Barad, phenomenon consists of a coming-together of the sound of screams, the materiality of tears, the hot, red face and tense body of the screaming child; the possible/probable anxiety of the baby's carer; and the transpersonal intensity of tension within the confined space itself. Not surprisingly, every participant who discussed such experiences noted the ability of these forces or intensities to generate anxiety. Participants recalled such events thus: 'You know what it's like, they suddenly lose it and they are inconsolable and being stuck on a bus where you can't get off because there is traffic, you just feel yourself panicking' (Mia). While another participant noted, 'I have taken her in the rush hour to West London to see my business partner a few weeks ago and I just left it a bit too late and got the train back about six, six thirty and it was just horrific and she was screaming her head off and there was commuters and I thought this is vile. . . . I am never doing this again' (Emma).

One factor which can make situations like this so 'vile' is distress about the crying child. Adding to this anxiety though is the anxiety about compromising the comfort of other passengers. As Sara Ahmed avers, this pressure to not disturb 'public comfort', or the comfort of strangers (Ahmed, 2010: 584), can exert a powerful force on how comfortable or uncomfortable one feels in a given setting. In a related vein, expressions of anxiety or discomfort being in confined public spaces with a crying baby were sometimes interwoven with feeling judged (and coming up wanting) as parents through subtle, non-verbal messages. As one participant put it, 'I always get the eyes from people, that: "Oh, my God, you are a parent with buggy, what are you thinking at this time of the day?"' (Eniko). In a similar vein another participant noted that 'in the early months of having a baby I felt . . . kind of at the mercies of people sort of judging you . . . on how good a job you are doing, and when you're on a train with a screaming child you know, and there is people sort of looking at you and whether they are parents or not kind of going: "can you get your child under control?" ' (Emma).

After Anderson, in these examples we see some of the ways that affects, temporalities, materialities and discourses about what constitutes 'good parenting' (and good mothering in particular) can come together to create intense feelings of discomfort for new mothers. This is based on subtle (and sometimes unsubtle) cues from those around them in spaces of public transport. They suggest discourses about maternal competency as relating to the ability to control the actions of others (Miller, 2005) and question the 'appropriateness' of babies (and caregiving more broadly) in certain places and times of day: all of which is sensed or intuited by new mothers and experienced as a transpersonal intensity. Whereas some scholarship has highlighted the role of transpersonal intensities in creating a sense of belonging in the city (e.g., Duff, 2010), these passages suggest how 'the felt feelings of others' can also lead to feeling *out* of place.[17]

A second kind of event which produced memorable transpersonal intensities was that of a baby being sick (vomiting) on a train. This scene was described thus: 'That was a grim journey. She was, yeah, she was sick, and there were quite a few people watching me as I cleaned up the floor of the train, the scabby floor of the train, with my muslin square. Yuck! Sodden muslin square' (Mary). While not as common as the experience of a baby crying, this event is significant for what it suggests about the role of (agentic) matter in experiences of early parenting. It shows the power of a baby's vomit – stinky, sticky and viscous – to act on the world around it, causing nearby passengers to shrink away. And it shows the capacity of the 'scabby' train floor to repel this mother as she cleans up the sick.

The juxtaposition of the *muslin square* – an object often used as a cuddle object by babies in the UK – and the *scabby floor* of the train again speaks of the discomfort felt by parents (and likely strangers) by the unavoidable folding-in of (nominatively) intimate forms of bodily care into public spaces – such as breastfeeding and nappy changing – that travelling with young babies can require. At the same time this comment also suggests how parenting in public can create opportunities to challenge and reshape received ways of relating to public space, as cleaning/caring for the floor of a train with one's own materials from home suggests.

On the other hand, in addition to the uncomfortable episodes described above participants spoke of positive experiences of public transport. For example, some noted the capacity of babies to transform the anonymous spaces of train and bus carriages into convivial spaces. One participant told of her baby 'making friends with everyone on the bus' (Carla), while another noted that 'it's quite fun if there are other children on the bus and they some-how . . . I don't know, they interact in their own way. It's quite funny' (Rosa). On this same theme a third participant observed:

Participant: I'm not someone who likes talking to people on the Tube or any-thing, but it's really strange because people will all look at you and the baby, and she's really social when she's looking round, and so people start talking to you, so that's quite a nice aspect of the journey.

Interviewer: Right, so it's become social in a way that it never was, yeah?

Participant: Yeah, definitely, yeah, because she forces it. I mean, if someone's reading their book she'll look at them until they give up and play with her, and it's nice, because you get everyone from old ladies to young teenage boys inter-acting with you. (Mary)[18]

This passage vividly illustrates the often-overlooked factor of infant agency: the ways babies themselves exert their will and desires in the world, as Louise Holt has noted (Holt, 2013). It shows how babies approach city life with a very different sense of sociability to that of adults and the potential for these alternatives to create unexpected (and often positive) affective atmospheres. Further, it shows some of the ways mother–baby assemblages can destabilise received understandings about ways of relating to others in public – in this case challenging the norm of noninteraction in spaces of public transport in the UK – in ways that new mothers enjoyed. Indeed each of the three events described in this section – crying, being sick and socialising with strangers – marks a kind of break or line of flight from normative ways of being, and affective atmospheres, in spaces of public transport. As these events have the power to create (sometimes extreme) discomfort to mothers and other pas-sengers, they can also create moments of unexpected joy.

Together these vignettes also echo a theme that runs through discussions with new parents about their sense of being in the world as no-longer-individuated, but rather shaped in and through the needs of (both human and non-human) others. These experiences echo themes discussed in chap-ter 1 about differences between parental and preparental selves. Regarding mobility, some of the participants in this study differentiated 'parents' from 'ordinary people' (suggesting how new motherhood can feel like a form of 'othering'), while others discussed the strangeness of 'switching camps', becoming 'one of the ones in the way'. To one participant, the disorientation of new parenthood was expressed thus:

Going down the market was always a bit . . . I felt really . . . yeah it (the pram) was just too wide and yeah it goes back to my earlier point about those few first weeks where you have this stark transition between your old life and your new life. I was used to just bombing down the market [*sic*] and getting a few bits and bobs and feeling like everybody else there, and actually *in the first few weeks you are not like everybody there,* and you can't get in with the buggy and you can't use it properly and you are perhaps resisting some . . . I was resisting my earlier stage of motherhood. (Emma, emphasis added)

Through these quotes we begin to get a sense of how transpersonal intensities which emanate through mother–baby assemblages can relate to processes of subject formation. As Anderson avers, affective atmospheres function as a 'shared ground from which subjective states and their attendant feelings and emotions emerge' (Anderson, 2009: 78). Through these vignettes we get a sense for how the 'felt-feelings of others' feed into processes by which new mothers come to understand themselves as such. Taken together, the experiences raised here reinforce the view of early motherhood as a period of metamorphosis as argued in chapter 1, a process of becoming something, and someone, different.

In drawing towards a conclusion to this chapter, I would like to hold two points in tension. On the one hand, as noted, journeys with babies can sometimes elicit pleasure and joy. Yet as this research suggests, the process of coming to know oneself as a mother can also entail feeling marked, 'othered' or out of place in spaces outside the home, where one's difference (both from one's former self and from others) is perceived affectively. Intimately bound up with this, the transition to motherhood involves care practices that include a range of different forms of emotional and physical labour. The joy they received from their babies and from the experience of becoming a mother was a powerful theme in this research. But at the same time, many participants also noted features that made this experience difficult (including sleep deprivation, coping with extended bouts of crying, problems with feeding, birth trauma and health problems, in addition to the struggles with mobility discussed here). In addition to a profound sense of joy, these experiences can lead to more difficult emotions such as frustration, uncertainty, guilt and other feelings.[19] This powerful mixture of emotions that can accompany the transition to motherhood marks this process as simultaneously positive and negative, and these intensities are often articulated through encounters with the social and material world.

CONCLUSION

Through an engagement with the New Materialism I have argued in this chapter that maternal subjectivity emerges out of entanglements with the more-than-human. This investigation advances scholarship in (and beyond) geography in three key ways. *First*, it advances conceptual work by showing how attending to the role of the more-than-human has the potential to generate richer and more comprehensive understandings of subjectivity by enabling an expanded understanding of agency. In so doing, I hope the work in this chapter and chapter one might help reinvigorate an area of geographical inquiry (in other words, the investigation of subjectivity) which has arguably languished in recent years. *Second*, it advances understanding about the geographies of motherhood by showing how mothers and babies, prams and other actors and actants come together as assemblages, producing both mobility and immobility. In turn, it shows some of the difficulties mother–baby–pram assemblages encounter in the course of journey-making, from the physical to the logistical to the affective. By attending to the transpersonal intensities produced through travelling with young babies, I hope to have shown how subtle reactions from members of the public can create environments which are off-putting to new mothers and serve as a disincentive to journeying outside the home. And *third*, it advances the mobilities literature by responding to the call to attend to affective and embodied aspects of day-to-day journey-making in order to analyse how experiences of journeying feed into the production of particular kinds of subjectivities.

At a finer grain of analysis, the concept of mother–baby–pram assemblages also highlights mobility's relational character. In moving with ones' baby, mothers move further away from their previous selves and forms of mobility towards new and much more relational forms. While mobility is typically positioned as a manifestation of independence, the accounts considered here highlight some of the many forms of mobility which do not fit this characterisation. Finally, I suggest that this work contributes to the growing body of scholarship on the role of 'parenting in public' within wider processes of the production of space. While travelling with a baby can sometimes create anxiety for new mothers, it can also create unexpected affordances and/or lines of flight from majoritarian spatial practice. While a crying baby on a train may create tension, a smiley, outgoing one has the power to break down walls of anonymity and fill a train carriage with joy. Likewise, using a muslin from home to swab a train floor can be read as activating a similarly unexpected kind of care relation with and for spaces of transport. These examples show the potential of parenting in public to 'make space otherwise'. I suggest that such an approach has the potential both to advance our understanding of care relations in the public realm (including with and for the more-than-human) and for reconceptualising the public sphere *as* a space of care in ways that bear further exploration.

NOTES

1. An earlier draft of this paper, co-authored with Justin Spinney, appeared in *Environment and Planning D, Society and Space* (2016), 34(6): 1113–1131. It is reprinted in modified form here with the publisher's kind permission.

2. This was in the context of an interview with novelist (and new mother) Chimamanda Adichie.

3. For a fuller discussion of this data set, please see chapter 1.

4. For example, over 80% of Americans become parents at some point in their lives. http://fatherhood.hhs.gov/charting02/introduction.htm#Who.

5. These data were collected by Justin Spinney and analysed by Justin and myself.

6. Please refer back to chapter 1 for a more detailed description of this methodology.

7. Though this is not to say that public transport in London could not be improved, as this chapter highlights.

8. Prams are wheeled devices used for transporting a baby. Babies in prams may be lying down, sitting up or (more often) slouching somewhere in-between. Prams come in a range of different designs (and prices).

9. See *After Kinship* for more on kinship objects.

10. Slings or baby 'wearing' is also associated with attachment parenting, though almost no participants in this study identified with this movement. Attachment parenting is associated with keeping one's baby physically close to the parent's body much of the time (as through sling-wearing, co-sleeping and breastfeeding).

11. Slings were also used in airplane journeys when hands were used to pull luggage.

12. Yet on this note, respondents also spoke of the physical strain that sling could inflict, through reference to sore backs, 'dodgy' knees and the like; while assembling with prams can be unwieldy, slings can take a higher physical toll.

13. Note that many pubs in Britain now serve coffee, tea and meals in addition to alcohol.

14. Baraitser makes a similar point, noting how objects and matter tend to come into view or become 'conspicuous' when they are ill-adapted or not fit for purpose (Baraitser, 2009: 135).

15. Though clearly there are also key ways in which these two forms of mobility diverge, in that in the case of parkour 'more difficult' forms of urban mobility are sought out (indeed they are purposefully created) as a pleasurable pursuit.

16. . . . and specifically the expectation that 'cumbersome' urban subjects give way to the unencumbered. See Buser et al. (2013) for more on lines of flight from majoritarian spatial practice.

17. See chapter 4 for a longer discussion about the relationships between public comfort, the felt feelings of others and mothering in public.

18. Though some parents in the UK will scold even young babies for staring at strangers, with admonishments of 'don't be nosey'.

19. For some the intensity of these feelings can lead to postnatal depression.

Chapter 3

Natureculture in the nursery: Lively breast milk, vibrant matter and the distributed agencies of infant feeding[1]

Chapter 2 put forward an argument about early motherhood as a relational practice that is achieved through engagements with human and non-human others. Extending that argument, this chapter brings together concerns with embodiment, materiality and maternal practice to consider the role of breast milk and other intracorporeal matter within breastfeeding assemblages.[2] By making a cut through these concerns, I seek to challenge commonly held understandings about the amount of control mothers have over infant feeding and breastfeeding by highlighting the role of biomatter within mothers' bodies in practices of infant feeding. I suggest that we can extend our understanding of breastfeeding by approaching the breastfeeding body as an *event* which is both dynamic and interacting (Grosz, 1994: 209). Employing this conceptual approach, I consider the role of biomatter within mothers' bodies in cases in which breastfeeding does not go to plan as a way to explore the politics of breast milk as agentic matter.

I explore the idea of breast milk as lively matter through engagements with posthumanist, new materialist and Deleuzo-Guattarian theory in order to produce a conceptualisation of motherhood and infant feeding in which agency is distributed. Such a conceptualisation allows us to give greater credence to the myriad ways the universe (after Karen Barad) 'acts back' against the things parents do in raising children, and specifically to recognise Hannah Stark's observation that 'the materiality of the body needs to be understood as a force that . . . shapes how we live in the world' (Stark, 2017: 66). Through this exploration I extend existing understandings of breastfeeding, care-work and the more-than-human and respond to Lisa Baraitser's call to attend to mothers' experiences of their own materiality (Baraitser, 2009: 150). In addition to these objectives, I seek to offer a critique of discourses which responsibilise and/or blame mothers for their supposed bodily 'inadequacies' in relation to their ability or non-ability to breastfeed (Hays, 1998; Warner, 2006).

This chapter has two parts. I first situate this investigation in relation to the relevant secondary literature and then trace out my conceptual framework. I then move on to consider some of the forces that breast milk and other kinds of biomatter can exert within mothers' bodies which can hinder breastfeeding. I do this by exploring instances in which mothers' bodies do not 'go along' with their plans for infant feeding, drawing on a selection of mothers' experiences with mastitis and blocked ducts drawn from the UK parenting website *mumsnet* and a selection of parenting blogs from the US.

I make three arguments in this chapter. First, I argue that biomatter and intracorporeal relations can play an important role in the events through which women come to understand themselves as mothers in the weeks and months post-birth. Second, I argue that considering breast milk as agentic matter usefully extends existing understandings of the concept of natureculture within and beyond the field of geography by approaching this concept through the intimate scale of the body. And third, I suggest that considering breast milk as agentic matter helps destabilise discourses which cast infant feeding as a question of (maternal) 'choice'. Most UK mothers report that they do not breastfeed as long as they would like (McAndrew et al., 2012). While successful breastfeeding can be hampered by lack of cultural and professional support as Bartlett (2003) and Smith et al. (2012) have argued, it can also – as I argue here – be constrained by intracorporeal forces within mothers' own bodies. Because the inability to breastfeed among mothers who desire to do so has been linked to increased risk of postnatal depression (Borra et al., 2015), this work thus adds to scholarship that seeks to 'shift blame off mothers' by highlighting the complex interplay of forces required to breastfeed successfully. In sum, in this chapter I argue that breastfeeding is an instance of distributed agency across human and non-human actors, thereby extending conceptual understanding of the role of the more-than-human (and breast milk specifically) within parenting and infant-feeding practices and making a political intervention in how both motherhood and infant feeding are understood.

SECONDARY LITERATURE AND CONCEPTUAL BACKGROUND

Considering breast milk as agentic matter extends existing scholarship along a number of lines. Within geography these include work on embodiment (Colls, 2007; Nast and Pile, 1998) and maternal bodies in particular (Longhurst, 2008), as noted in the introduction. Further, it also builds on the growing body of scholarship on the spatial, affective and material practices involved in the formation of parental and maternal identities, as discussed in chapter 1 (Aitken, 2000; Dowling, 2000; Holloway, 1998; Luzia, 2010; Madge and O'Connor, 2005; Pain, 2001; Rose, 2004), and the concept of breastfeeding as an assemblage composed of human and non-human components as discussed in chapter 2. It also extends work on how parenting practice is shaped in and through engagements with the non-human, such as second-hand baby things (Waight, 2014), 'family' cars (Waitt and Harada, 2016) and prams and built form as discussed in chapter 2.

Through its focus on the politics of biomatter though, this work perhaps builds most directly on scholarship on the fleshy and fluidic geographies of materials that transgress and destabalise the body boundary as with blood donation, stem cell preservation and placentas (Boyer, 2010; Colls and Fannin, 2013; Copeman, 2009; Fannin, 2013; Hall, 2000; Longhurst, 2001; Waldby and Mitchell, 2006). This scholarship has highlighted a number of important findings. The work of Colls and Fannin has shown how the placenta destabilises taken-for-granted understandings of the body boundary, exploring how this (temporary) organ allows us to think about bodies, relations between interior and exterior and self and other in new ways (Colls and Fannin, 2013), responding to Hannah Stark's call to attend to the 'forces . . . which both form and undermine subjectivity and which occur at scales both larger and smaller than the human' (Stark, 2017: 109). It has shown how biomatter is capable of undergoing cultural reclassification from a low-value substance to a high-value one, as has happened with stem cells (Fannin, 2013). It has shown how blood donation can serve as a site of cultural transformation (Copeman, 2009), and that expressed breast milk can function as a means of extending the boundaries of the self (Boyer, 2010). Yet while generating a range of useful insights into how breast milk and other forms of biomatter can be understood, this body of scholarship does not consider breast milk – or other bodily effluvia – as agentic matter in its own right, or examine the politics of how such an interpretation might reframe discourses around motherhood and infant feeding.

Towards putting this discussion in a broader context, it is also worth noting that breast milk is a highly politicised form of matter about which there are divergent views. Similar to other bodily substances that transgress the body boundary, breast milk is sometimes vilified. Building on Mary Douglas's thesis that matter which escapes the body is coded as unclean, offensive and dangerous (Douglas, 1966), Aimee Grant has shown the disgust over breast milk in the context of breastfeeding in public that has been expressed in reader comments in the UK's most-read online newspaper, the tabloid *The Mail Online* (Grant, 2016). Along similar lines Longhurst (2001), Grosz (1994) and Bartlett (2005) have argued that breast milk is additionally problematic within misogynist cultures as it represents women's biological productivity.

Yet while breast milk is sometimes vilified as a target of disgust, breast-feeding is also the iconic form of giving comfort, succour and nourishment (Hausman, 2003). Breast milk is at the heart of powerful messages about the preferred form of infant feeding, and raising breastfeeding rates has been identified as a key step in reducing health inequalities in the UK. Among health professionals and advocates for women's and child's health breast milk is the undisputed best form of infant feeding in terms of health benefits for mothers and children (Rollins et al., 2016; Victora et al., 2016). Breast milk has been shown to reduce the risk of diarrhoea, allergies and sudden infant death syndrome (cot death) when babies are small, as well as to reduce chances of getting diabetes, leukaemia, lymphoma and asthma as children grow older (Goldman, 2000). Julie Smith avers that 'human milk should be viewed as "broad-spectrum medicine" as well as nutrition' (Smith, 2004: 371), while Jacqueline Wolf has noted that 'few activities in life have the potential to contribute as much to the health of women and children as breast-feeding' (Wolf, 2006: 397).

Moreover breast milk includes antibodies, enzymes and hormones such as oxytocin which scientists do not yet know how to replicate.[3] Breast milk thus delivers not only nutritional but also immunological, affective and other health benefits to both mothers and children (Goldman, 2000; Scariati et al., 1997; Victora et al., 2016). It lowers the risk of ear, lower-respiratory tract, urinary tract and other kinds of infections in babies, while reducing the risk of breast cancer later in life for mothers (Gartner et al., 2005).[4] It reduces instances of vomiting and the chances of catching pneumonia.[5] Indeed it is estimated that if breastfeeding rates were to increase to near-universal levels worldwide, it would prevent 823,000 deaths of children under five annually and lead to a reduction of 20,000 deaths due to breast cancer (Victora et al., 2016). Breast milk is thus recognised as the ideal food for babies in both rich and poor countries by every major health organisation worldwide,[6] and this is even recognised by the infant formula industry (Boyer, 2010).[7]

Nevertheless, views on breast milk itself vary widely. Towards understanding these diverging views, it can be useful to refer to the work of Waldby and Mitchell in their book *Tissue Economies: Blood, Organs and Cell Lines in Late Capitalism* (2006). Waldby and Mitchell argue that understandings of biosubstances such as blood, stem cells and organs shift between 'waste', 'gift' and 'commodity', sometimes reflecting mixtures of all three. (They further argue that it is through biomatter that has gained value within fields of disease treatment and experimentation that the framing of 'commodity' is most pronounced.) Given breast milk's disease-fighting properties, together with its imbrication within both systems of donation and bioindustry,[8] I suggest that Waldby and Mitchell's analysis provides a useful framework to understand the varying and shiftable ways breast milk is currently viewed throughout many parts of the industrialised West. At the same time I suggest that the arguments in this chapter extend Waldby and Mitchell's analysis by opening a space in which to consider biomatter itself as an actor within the networks in which it circulates. Having outlined how this chapter advances existing scholarship on breast milk, I will now trace out my conceptual framework.

Conceptual framework

Like chapter 2, my conceptual framework in this chapter draws on scholarship from the New Materialism as a way to highlight the role of material agency within maternal practice. After Deleuze I conceptualise the body as a series of ongoing events and am guided by the question 'what can a body do'? (rather than 'what it means') (Bray and Colebrook, 1998: 36; Deleuze and Guattari, 2004). Within Deleuzian philosophy 'bodies' do not necessarily refer (only) to human bodies, but rather to beings or entities coming together to achieve something. Such bodies are always constituted through the relations they form with others (Stark, 2017: 71). This can mean human bodies in their interactions with one another and with the non-human, but it can also refer to machines. In this analysis it so happens that actual human bodies *are* the locus of analysis but with a focus on the intracorporeal interactions and processes.

As noted in the previous chapter, new materialist social theory seeks to analyse the politics of materiality and material agency together with the ways matter and systems of representation relate to one another (Alaimo and Hekman, 2008; Barad, 2007; Braidotti, 2002; Colebrook, 2008; Coole and Frost, 2010; Van der Tuin and Dolphijn, 2012). This body of work has come out of a wide-ranging multidisciplinary engagement across the humanities, social sciences and physical sciences to explore the politics of more-than-human agency and the effects of such agency on traditional understandings of humanism. As noted in the introduction, new materialist philosophy seeks to deconstruct conceptual boundaries between subjects and objects and between bodies and matter by attending to what Karan Barad calls 'agential intra-action' (Barad, 2008: 132). This concept is the idea that entities make one another through their relations with each other: in other words, entities are not ontologically prior but rather are in a state of constant (co)-becoming through their myriad relations with other entities.

Combining a Deleuzian approach to the body with a recognition of the role of the more-than-human in constituting (and destabilising the primacy of) human subjects, Bray and Colebrook suggest approaching the body as 'a negotiation with images . . . pleasures, pains, other bodies, space, visibility and medical practice' (Bray and Colebrook, 1998: 43). In this way they highlight the ways bodies are both dynamic and constituted in relation to 'things' commonly thought of as either within or beyond them. In a related vein Rosi Braidotti suggests conceptualising the body as a 'field of intersecting material and symbolic forces' (Braidotti, 2002: 25). Drawing on these frameworks, this analysis seeks to extend understandings of mothering and maternal subjects through a consideration of 'what breastmilk does', endevouring, after Coole and Frost, to '(take) seriously the material intricacies of existence' (Coole and Frost, 2010: 32).

As noted in chapter 2, the New Materialism has been taken up in geography both as a means of theorising more-than-human agency in the context of the Anthropocene and as a way to destabilise nature-culture binaries (Anderson and Perrin, 2015; Castree and Nash, 2006; Kirsch, 2013; Tolia-Kelly, 2013; Whatmore, 2013). As Anderson and Perrin note, this turn has taken place in the context of a broader concern in (and beyond) the discipline of geography with posthumanism, that is, the 'widespread, and now increasingly "materialist" concern within the humanities (and social sciences) to move beyond the legacy of a narrow, humanist conception of culture as something separate from, and elevated above, the natural world. Countering the idea that humans occupy a separate and privileged place among other beings' (Anderson and Perrin, 2015: 1). As Castree and Nash note, the ways we now recognise human-nature interdependence have 'disturb(ed) an idealized definition of the human subject as separate and liberated from nature and fully in command of self and non-human others' (Castree and Nash, 2006: 501). This turn has led to the emergence of the concept of 'natureculture' as a means of recognising both more-than-human agency and the lack of ontological distinction between the two concepts.

To date the theorisation of agentic matter and more-than-human agency has focused largely on issues of environmental sustainability (Whatmore, 2013); animal geographies (Whatmore, 2006); embodiment (Colls, 2007; Roe and Greenhough, 2006); food and eating (Anderson, 2014); and urban form (Latham and McCormack, 2004; Simpson, 2013). Tolia-Kelly has flagged up the importance of interrogating the political implications of our intra-actions with the more-than-human (Tolia-Kelly, 2013), while Kirsch warns against making assumptions about which sort of more-than-human matter will play a key role in a given event (Kirsch, 2013).

This chapter furthers our understanding of what Braun has called our emerging 'modalities of posthumanism' (Braun, 2004) by extending scholarship on the body and intracorporeal matter as an important prism through which to explore the concept of natureculture. Building on Rachael Colls's exploration of body fat as agentic matter, I consider breast milk as a means to advance understanding of the 'dynamism of bodily matter' (Colls, 2007: 354). In the rest of this chapter, I analyse how breast milk relates to the socially situated bodies in which it is made by examining the flows and blockages of breast milk. In turn I explore the capacity of breast milk itself as an agentic force within breastfeeding assemblages, and some of the kinds of intra-actions that occur between breast milk and the lactating women in whose bodies it is produced. I explore the relationships between the desires of mothering subjects and those of the biomaterial systems that produce breast milk by exploring cases in which different 'parts' of the maternal body essentially act against one other in cases of blocked ducts and mastitis. As such this chapter directly responds to Colls and Fannin's call to consider the body as relational space (Colls and Fannin, 2013).

AGENTIC BREAST MILK

Having outlined how this work sits disciplinarily and traced out my conceptual framework, I will now turn to explore 'what breast milk does'. I will first briefly outline the process by which breast milk is produced and (normally) leaves the body once produced and then turn to consider cases in which this event is interrupted. Taken together, breast milk, hormones, muscles, nerves, other biomatter within the mother's body, 'the (agentic) mother herself' and a nursing baby, babies or young child constitute an excellent example of agental intra-action between a range of biomaterially entangled and mutually affecting phenomena. The process by which milk is produced in the body (lactogenesis) consists of several stages, beginning during pregnancy when mammary glands begin to release colostrum in preparation for breastfeeding (Edgar and Sebring, 2005). After the placenta is delivered during birth, levels of progesterone (which inhibit the production of milk during pregnancy) drop suddenly, and at this point milk normally begins to be produced in the alveoli (tiny sacs in the breasts) (Edgar and Sebring, 2005). In established breastfeeding (after the first few days) a baby's sucking stimulates nerves in the breast which signal the hypothalamus to release prolactin and oxytocin from the pituitary gland. The release of oxytocin causes the muscles surrounding the alveoli to contract, forcing milk from the alveoli through the milk ducts and out the nipple (this process is called the let-down reflex) (Edgar and Sebring, 2005).

In addition to these processes taking place inside the body, breast milk intra-acts with forces outside the body in a number of ways. Not only is the let-down reflex activated in response to stimuli outside the body from the baby, but breast milk also changes composition based on the health of the mother, for example, delivering antibodies to the baby for any colds the mother catches.[9] Breast milk carries with it the flavours of food the mother eats (Mennella and Beauchamp, 1991); changes composition based on local atmospheric conditions,[10] time of day and age of the baby; and delivers a different nutrient mix as babies age in response to what is needed at a given developmental stage (Brown, forthcoming; Prentice et al., 1981; Tomori, forthcoming). Breast milk carries biomarkers of the woman producing it, and in turn its departure from the body (whether through breastfeeding or expressing) delivers a modicum of protection against breast cancer and osteoporosis for the woman in whose body it was produced. Breastfeeding can even shape the mood of mothers and babies as breast milk contains oxytocin, the hormone which produces feelings of trust and well-being (Ishak, 2011; Lane et al., 2013).

Thinking more expansively, breast milk also relates to public health campaigns which raise awareness about the benefits of breastfeeding, media representations and public discussion relating to breastfeeding, as well as artefacts/non-human actors such as nipple guards, nipple cream (in the case of cracked nipples), breast pads, nursing bras and breast pumps. It relates to bodily knowledge which mothers who seek to breastfeed must acquire about how to put the baby to the breast so that he or she will be able to successfully feed (latching on), as well as to the health professionals, lactation consultants, friends, online videos, blogs, books or magazines which are used to gain this knowledge. Breast milk can even be seen to relate to friends and family members of the breastfeeding mother in terms of how well (or poorly) they support her in her efforts to breastfeed as long as she wants to, together with social mores about breastfeeding which may affect how comfortable mothers feel breastfeeding in different locales or breastfeeding an older baby or young child.

In all of these respects breastfeeding (and maternal practice more generally) can be understood as an event or assemblage, involving multiple human actors and non-human actants. Breastfeeding draws together the biomaterial, the symbolic, the cognitive (in terms of information about breastfeeding's benefits), the emotional and the biomechanical (both in terms of embodied learning on the part of the lactating mother about the logistics of latching on and in terms of the intracorporeal events required to breastfeed that were outlined earlier). Breastfeeding is also an excellent example of the Deleuzian body marked by relationality in that breastfeeding assemblages are composed of corporeal, affective and material relations not only between mothers and babies and babies and breast milk but also between mothers and their milk in terms of changing milk composition in response to the mother's physical health and between breast milk, mothers and broader socio-technical, material-discursive and affective environments. In all these ways breastfeeding assemblages challenge binarised understandings of 'nature' and 'culture', showing how these elements are in no way distinguishable or mutually exclusive.

Within these assemblages I suggest that breast milk functions as active, lively matter. I suggest that it can be seen to possess what Jane Bennett terms 'self-directing activeness' (Bennett, 2010: 53) in that, barring complications, it 'wants' to leave the body: seeking to fulfil an objective outside the body in which it has been made and inside the body of another. Yet despite breast milk's desire (if you will) to leave the body, it is not always able to. In cases where breast milk is *not* able to traverse the body boundary, it can result in physical pain in the form of blocked ducts, in which milk effectively 'gets stuck' in the milk ducts causing engorgement and mastitis, which can be caused by milk seeping out from the ducts into the bloodstream, causing infection. Let us now briefly turn to consider such cases as a means to 'see' breast milk's agentic force.

Although for some breastfeeding can bring with it confidence and feelings of pride and accomplishment regarding what one's body can do (Dykes, 2003), pain is also a feature of some mothers' experiences of breastfeeding. In fact pain is the second-most common reason given among UK mothers who stop breastfeeding in the first few weeks post-birth (McAndrew et al., 2012: 106). And although most mothers in the UK stop breastfeeding within the first four weeks post-birth, 60% of mothers who breastfeed to eight months or longer report experiencing breast or nipple pain at some point.[11] Twenty-six per cent of all UK mothers who breastfeed eight months experience either blocked ducts or mastitis, bringing with it flu-like symptoms that can include chills, fever, body pain, nausea and fatigue in addition to breast pain (McAndrew et al., 2012: 109).

As Williamson, Leeming and others have shown (Williamson et al., 2012) problems with breastfeeding can come as a surprise to new mothers. While some mothers may begin to think about the practical aspects of breastfeeding before birth, many are so focused on getting through the birth itself that they do not spend significant amounts of time thinking about how they might respond to issues that might arise relating to infant feeding. As parenting blogger Meredith Band noted on her entry entitled 'Mastitis and Me' in the parenting blog *mommyish*, 'There are a lot of things to worry about when you're pregnant. Most of those involve how the baby is going to leave your body. I didn't give a lot of thought to what would be going on with my body after giving birth'.[12] Some women are able to resolve physical problems related to breastfeeding by taking antibiotics (in the case of mastitis) or by learning different physical techniques to unblock ducts. NHS guidelines suggest using compresses, taking ibuprofen, massage and hot baths or showers and expressing milk regularly in order to alleviate the symptoms of engorged breasts and/or mastitis.[13]

We can gain further insight into mothers' experiences of mastitis from comments posted on the popular UK parenting website *mumsnet*.[14] As a review of anonymous posts on the non-password-protected site in 2005 (N:36)[15] together with selected parenting blogs, reveals, some women also find techniques of 'combing' breasts with fingers or a wide-toothed comb along duct gland lines (to relieve blocked ducts) successful in alleviating breast pain. Mothers also 'act back' against breast pain by using microwavable flannel or cloth sacks filled with rice or experiment with different feeding positions (including feeding lying down with the baby's legs up towards their shoulders as a position that some found successful in relieving blocked ducts,[16] positioning the baby's nose towards the sore area).[17] These techniques are just some of the many forms of bodywork women must learn in order to manage their changing bodies through pregnancy and new motherhood, as Longhurst (2008) has noted.

However, as comments on the *mumsnet* bulletin board and other parenting blogs reveal, some mothers are not able to resolve pain related to breastfeeding in these ways. Some do not receive support (from lactation consultants, other health professionals or even knowledgeable friends) that might help them overcome physical barriers, and for others the physical pain itself is simply too overwhelming. Commentators describe mastitis as 'absolutely dreadful'. One contributor remarked that she felt like she had been 'set about with a baseball bat', while another observed simply: 'Oh my God, there's nothing like the pain of mastitis!'[18] Similar sentiments are echoed in the American parenting blog *babycenter* in the comment: 'There was also a sudden onset of intense pain in the outer area/armpit area of my left breast. I didn't realize how bad it was until an hour later I was violently, uncontrollably shaking from the chills'.[19] Similarly, as American mum Tal Gooden noted in the *Huffington Post* of her experience with mastitis: 'I was terrified as I felt hard lumps in my right breast. The skin on my breast had red splotches and felt unusually warm to the touch. I could barely lift my arm or lie down without feeling excruciating pain. In addition to feeling sore, I also began to battle fatigue, fever, and nausea. I didn't know what was happening to me'.[20] Some *mumsnet* comments were sarcastic, as in the query: 'Any tips on how to "firmly massage" my boob when I can hardly bear to touch it?' and even irreverent: 'My boobs are just crap! If they had their way I think they'd just want to be sex objects'.[21]

Lighthearted quips notwithstanding, the general tenor of commentary on this *mumsnet* thread was summed up in the poignant observation that 'people underestimate how awful mastitis makes you feel'. This sentiment is echoed in the broader parenting blogosphere, articulated by American mum Meredith Band in the blog *mommyish* of her experience with mastitis that 'trying to rub those knots out was, without a doubt, one of the most painful experiences of my life. It wasn't always easy to convince myself to do it while my body screamed "Why are we doing this to us?!" '[22] These comments resonate with

Catherine Robinson's work on women's experiences of pain during breast-feeding (and in turn feelings of loss and guilt) among mothers who want to breastfeed but are unable, owing to the way breastfeeding is positioned as the ideal or aspirational feeding choice (Robinson, 2016).[23]

Through these cases we can see how the process of lactogenesis, or the production of milk within the body, can lead to a range of different outcomes. It might lead to successful breastfeeding, bringing comfort and satiation for baby and a sense of peace for the mother. Or it might lead to blocked ducts, engorgement or an infection bringing with it chills, fatigue and nausea and distress for the mother, as well as distress for the (hungry) baby. I suggest that through these cases we can also see breast milk as a form of matter which is dynamic with its own vital force, and which 'comes to matter' through its relations with other phenomena (e.g., milks ducts and the muscle that surrounds them, lactating mothers and their babies). In this way, through these cases we see breast milk's liveliness, how it functions (after Colls) as a 'form of bodily matter that is not only impinged upon by outside forces but has its own capacities to act and be active' (Colls, 2007: 358).

In turn, through the experiences of mastitis and blocked ducts considered here, we are also able to see some of the ways biomatter and intracorporeal relations can shape the processes by which women come to understand themselves as mothers in the weeks and months post-birth (although not in a deterministic way). For some the experience of managing mastitis or blocked ducts leads to new forms of embodied knowledge, such as through learning the technique of breast combing to break up a block or finding a new way to position one's baby to encourage milk to flow. For others, however, the physical pain of mastitis and/or blocked ducts may lead to stopping breast-feeding and (for some) feelings of guilt or sadness about that eventuality, as the literature has described (Robinson, 2016).

CONCLUSION

In this chapter I have put forward a conceptualisation of breastfeeding as an assemblage in which agency is diffused across different human and non-human actors. I have argued for an understanding of breastfeeding not only as a case of distributed agency but also as a case of distributed *intracorporeal* agency, thus responding to Colls and Fannin's provocation to consider the body as relational space. I have argued this through a consideration of cases of mastitis and blocked ducts as instances in which the different agential forces within breastfeeding assemblages are in conflict with one another. In such cases a mother's desire to breastfeed is in tension with forces within her body that seek otherwise. As such this work challenges notions of the coherent enlightenment subject by showing how mothers' very bodies can be the site of multiple (sometimes conflicting) agencies. A given mother may want to breastfeed, but her body may have (metaphorically speaking) other plans, showing how the body is, after Braidotti, 'an assemblage of forces' (Braidotti, 2002: 104). In turn, a mother experiencing mastitis and/or blocked ducts may be able to resolve physical problems, or she may not. I therefore suggest that in addition to the ways in which women's (would be) 'choice' to breastfeed is constrained by social and cultural factors (e.g., lack of appropriate support and nonacceptance of breastfeeding in public) (Bartlett, 2002; Smith et al., 2012), it can also be constrained by intracorporeal forces within her own body.

Through this analysis I have sought to advance scholarship on embodiment, material agency, human–non-human relations and geographies of motherhood. I have considered some of the different kinds of bodywork and forms of embodied knowledge that emerge through bodily intra-actions for breastfeeding women (e.g., breast combing and massage). Drawing on concepts from feminist and new materialist philosophy, I have argued that matter and events taking place within the body have an important role to play in processes by which mothers come to know themselves as such. I have advanced a consideration of breast milk's agentic nature and suggested a conceptualisation of breastfeeding as an achievement realised through ongoing negotiations with the non-human.

Through a focus on breast milk inside the body, I hope to have suggested that breast milk and the women in whose bodies it is produced not only intra-act but literally co-make one another, with maternal health influencing the composition of breast milk and the production of breast milk conferring health benefits – and sometimes pain – for the woman in whose body it is made. And following on from this, I suggest that attending to these kinds of bodily intra-actions helps advance our understanding of the concept of natureculture at the intimate scale of the body.

Finally, beyond these conceptual objectives I hope that a greater recognition of the myriad bodily forces and forms of agency involved in breastfeeding might also help mothers who find breastfeeding difficult or impossible. To return to mothers who stop breastfeeding sooner than they planned due to physical problems or pain, I hope that highlighting breast milk's agentic nature might have a political dividend as a means to combat feelings of guilt or grief and help destabilise narratives which overemphasise maternal choice in infant-feeding decisions. And likewise, to governments which seek to raise their breastfeeding rates, I hope this analysis highlights one of the many dimensions in which mothers need more and better support in order to fulfil their own wishes regarding breastfeeding.

NOTES

1. I would like to thank Annmarie Mol for her useful comments on an earlier draft of this chapter given at the Emotional Geographies Conference in Groningen, Netherlands, in 2013.

2. For a description of how I use the concept of assemblage, please see chapter 2.

3. American Academy of Pediatrics website: https://www.healthychildren.org/English/ages-stages/baby/breastfeeding/Pages/Breastfeeding-Benefits-Your-Babys-Immune-System.aspx. Accessed 10/3/2017.

4. For more information see also the US Department of Health and Human Services: http://www.womenshealth.gov/breastfeeding. Accessed 4/3/2017.

5. American Academy of Pediatrics website: https://www.healthychildren.org/English/ages-stages/baby/breastfeeding/Pages/Breastfeeding-Benefits-Your-Babys-Immune-System.aspx. Accessed 10/3/2017.

6. NHS recommendations echo UNICEF and WHO guidelines which recommend that breast milk should be the only food infants receive for the first six months of life. http://www.nhs.uk/Conditions/pregnancy-and-baby/Pages/why-breastfeed.aspx#close. Accessed 20/6/2014. See also: World Health Organization (2003). *Global Strategy for Infant and Young Child Feeding*. Geneva, Switzerland: World Health Organization, UNICEF ISBN 92–4–156221–8.

7. Although formula companies also habitually undermine this message in their advertising and marketing.

8. For an example of an industry which uses human milk, see Prolacta Bioscience at http://prolacta.uk.

9. American Academy of Pediatrics website: https://www.healthychildren.org/English/ages-stages/baby/breastfeeding/Pages/Breastfeeding-Benefits-Your-Babys-Immune-System.aspx. Accessed 10/3/2017.

10. For example, breast milk has lower fat content in summer months in order to deliver more hydration.

11. This rate is significantly below NHS guidelines. Reasons why breastfeeding rates in the UK are so low will be addressed in more detail in chapters 4 and 5.

12. http://www.mommyish.com/2014/11/12/my-experience-with-mastitis/. Accessed 10/3/2017.

13. http://www.nhs.uk/Conditions/Mastitis/Pages/Treatment.aspx. Accessed 10/3/2017.

14. Please see chapter 1 for a consideration of *mumsnet* as a source. As noted, to protect the privacy of posters I have removed post dates and posters' names and obtained permission to reprint these posts from *mumsnet*.

15. http://www.mumsnet.com/Talk/breast_and_bottle_feeding/73762-mastitis-experiences-please/AllOnOnePage. Accessed 11/3/2016.

16. http://www.mumsnet.com/Talk/breast_and_bottle_feeding/73762-mastitis-experiences-please/AllOnOnePage. Accessed 11/3/2016.

17. https://blog.mothersboutique.com/experiences-of-mastitis/. Accessed 10/3/2017.

18. http://www.mumsnet.com/Talk/breast_and_bottle_feeding/73762-mastitis-experiences-please/AllOnOnePage. Accessed 11/3/2016. As noted in chapter 1, in addition to not including post date, posts have been paraphrased or minimally altered to protect posters' identities.

19. https://community.babycenter.com/post/a31797461/mastitis_experiences_at_6_weeks_pp_right_now. Accessed 10/3/2017.

20. http://www.huffingtonpost.com/tai-gooden/breastfeeding-woes-my-exp_b_5711979.html. Accessed 12/3/2017.

21. http://www.mumsnet.com/Talk/breast_and_bottle_feeding/73762-mastitis-experiences-please/AllOnOnePage. Accessed 11/3/2016.

22. http://www.mommyish.com/2014/11/12/my-experience-with-mastitis/. Accessed 10/3/2017.

23. Johnson's work also resonates with research showing a link between the incidence of postnatal depression and the inability to breastfeed among mothers who want to (Borra et al., 2015).

Chapter 4

Breastfeeding in public: Affect, public comfort and the agency of strangers[1]

As the previous chapter explored the role of breast milk itself within breast-feeding assemblages, this chapter and the next turn to look at the role of mothers' interactions in public space in the course of breastfeeding.[2] Empirically it draws on women's experiences breastfeeding outside the home in South East England based on data collected between 2008 and 2009. Its aims are threefold. First, it increases understanding regarding an issue of direct importance to health policy, in terms of why Britain has some of the lowest breastfeeding duration rates in the industrialised West.[3] Second, it highlights some of the ways more-than-visual affective environments can shape and constrain health-promoting behaviours. Third, it extends conceptual work relating to corporeal practice and urban materiality more broadly through an analysis of the relationships between affect, embodiment and the limits of sociability.

Research is based on a mixed-method qualitative analysis of eleven interviews, a forty-six-person survey of new mothers' experiences breastfeeding in public conducted in Southampton, Hampshire, between 2008 and 2009, and a patent application for a 'portable lactation module'. Approaching these data through an engagement with the work of cultural theorist Sara Ahmed, I show how the limits of belonging for breastfeeding women in public space can be marked through affective practice, with implications for how, where and how long UK women breastfeed.

I suggest that Sara Ahmed's work on collective feelings, public comfort and concepts of the 'killjoy' (2004, 2010a, 2010b, 2008) and 'affect alien' (2010b) provides a useful means to think through the ways affective practice can exclude as well as connect and help explain the discomfort many women feel breastfeeding in public in the UK. The killjoy is someone whose presence makes others uncomfortable (sometimes without even opening their mouth), while to be an affect 'alien' is to have the sense that one is feeling the wrong thing (Ahmed, 2010). Ahmed suggests that concepts of the killjoy and the affect alien can serve as ways to highlight the exclusions and violences on which certain forms of happiness and types of comfort depend. As Ahmed notes, 'The mere proximity of some bodies involves an affective conversion. We learn . . . how histories are condensed in the very intangibility of an atmosphere, or in *the tangibility of the bodies that seem to get in the way*' (Ahmed, 2010: 584, emphasis added).[4]

The idea that certain bodies 'get in the way' (materially, symbolically or both) disrupting the comfort of others harmonises nicely with the work of a small number of geographers whose work concerns the intersections of affect and corporeality. This includes the work of Rachel Colls (2006) and Robyn Longhurst (2000, 2008), who have examined the cultural politics associated with 'overweight' and pregnant bodies. By highlighting the anxieties over excess, effluvia, self-control and subjectivity that particular bodies can generate, this work has highlighted the way that difference is materially and affectively experienced as well as socially constructed.[5] These anxieties relate closely to breastfeeding. As noted in the previous chapter, while revered by some for its unique health and immunological benefits for both mother and baby,[6] breastfeeding can also raise deep-seated anxieties about (any) bodily fluid which transgresses the body boundary and becomes mobile (Boyer, 2010; Hausman, 2003; Longhurst, 2000; Waldby and Mitchell, 2006).

Building on this work I argue that despite being promoted by policy, breastfeeding women are marked and marginalised in the public sphere in the UK through a process of intersubjective affective practice. Drawing on Ahmed, I propose that breastfeeding women are expected to act so as to maintain public comfort (i.e., the comfort of others) or risk censure. I further argue that this schema is sustained in the way breastfeeding is provisioned-for in the built environment in the form of lactation rooms. I suggest that these spaces, practices and affective environments can serve to constrain women in the UK from breastfeeding in public. In turn, I argue that an analysis of these practices, space and affects can help explain why UK breastfeeding duration rates might be so low when viewed in a global comparative context.

The chapter is divided into four parts. After a brief review of the relevant secondary literature and policy context, I outline the methods used in this study. I then analyse findings in two themed sections. The first of these focuses on the subtle and sometimes overt forms of social regulation that can mark and marginalise women breastfeeding in space outside the home in the contemporary UK, and the second examines how built form can collude with this process.

BACKGROUND

This chapter draws on two broad fields of academic literature: one that concerns the relations between corporeality, materiality and urban subjectivity and the other on the embodied politics of breastfeeding. It is also situated within a policy context which explicitly seeks to raise breastfeeding rates as a matter of improving public health and reducing health inequalities.[7] What follows is a selective reading of each of these fields, drawing out key themes as they relate most closely to this work.

As noted, conceptually this work is situated within the rise in interest in corporeality and materialism that has occurred throughout the human and social sciences in recent years. Within geography this turn has been most clearly visible in the work of cultural geographers and others interested in nonrepresentational theory. This work is marked by a concern with practice and an interest in how the visceral, sensual, instinctive and affective dimensions of social life are generated and move between human and non-human actors and actants (Lorimer, 2008: 552; see also Popke, 2009). Work in this vein focusing on corporeal practice and urban materiality specifically has been interested in the way that affects connect people, such as through sociability, solidarity (Latham, 2003) and joy (Dewsbury, 2000). This work has served as an energising force for the discipline as a whole. Yet it has also been criticised by Geographers of different stripe for failing to attend to how identity-based power asymmetries can shape and constrain corporeal practice (Saldanha, 2005; Sharp, 2009; Thien, 2005; Tolia-Kelly, 2006).[8] Saldanha (2005) has expressed particular concern that this occlusion limits the ability of non-representational theory (NRT) informed approaches to adequately address how power relations are produced (and consolidated) through lived practice.

The concern is that by focusing on – indeed, arguably celebrating – expressions of individual freedom (see Latham [2003] and Latham and McCormack [2004], for examples) without attending to the identity-politics which prefigure those freedoms is to ignore the extensive body of scholarship establishing the difference that *difference* makes in understanding subjectivity.[9] Periscoping out to a critique of current work in cultural geography more broadly, Tolia-Kelly warns that these oversights risk creating 'a gap between our claims and our interface with "real policy", "lived environments" and "public geographies"' (Tolia-Kelly, 2010: 359, drawing on Fuller, 2008). This work seeks to help redress this.

Relatedly, this investigation also builds on and extends scholarship in and beyond geography on embodiment, subjectivity and the politics of public space (Chouinard, 2004; Colls, 2006; Longhurst, 2000, 2008; Moss and Dyck, 2003; Watson, 2006). Work in this field owes a debt to a long line of scholarship stretching back to the 1990s when, through engagements with feminist and poststructuralist theories, Geographers began exploring ideas of identity as performed (Butler, 1993) and concepts of bodies and cities as dynamic and mutually constitutive (Grosz, 1998). This scholarship has highlighted the power of intersecting, identity-based systems of social differentiation (e.g., race, class, gender, sexual orientation and disability) to mark and marginalise subjects in the urban realm (Kobayashi and Peake, 2000; Massey, 1993; Ray and Rose, 2000; Ruddick, 1996; Wilson, 1991).

Taking such concerns forward, scholarship in this area has clearly established how processes of creating social difference are bound up with gendered, racialised and sexualised politics of visuality that are enacted through practices of looking and being looked at (Buck-Morss, 1989; Foley et al., 2007; Irigaray, 1985; Rose, 1993; Wilson, 1992). These analyses call attention to the pleasure and power that looking confers on the (typically heterosexual, middle-class, white male) subject and the feelings of discomfort and/or disempowerment it can produce for the object of that gaze (typically women). Characterised by a sexualised desire to possess or consume, the concept of the male gaze has informed scholarship on urban citizenship by differentiating subjects who can – and cannot – move through the city unremarked upon, signalling the privilege that subject position entails (epitomised by the archetypal figure of the flâneur).

This chapter extends existing work in this field in two ways. First, it provides a fuller understanding of the sensate aspects of corporeal experience, particularly the ways that apprehensions about mood and (after Ahmed) the 'intangibility of atmosphere' can generate feelings of being out of place. As such this work helps develop understanding about the more-than-visual aspects of urban subjectivity and bodily experience. Second, it highlights a form of exclusion that cuts across a broad category of urban subjects. In some respects the UK has better levels of gender equity than it did twenty years ago. Women in the UK (particularly white and middle-class women) have better access to the employment market, better wages relative to their male counterparts and more opportunities to combine wage-work with care-work than they did even in 1990s. However, within this broader landscape of increased access and equity, various forms of gender-based marginalisation and socio-spatial exclusion persist. This can be seen in the public culture of sexism that includes street harassment and the sale of pornography at high-street news agents, as well as cultures of toxic masculinity and 'lad culture' that are threaded through UK society (Bates, 2016; Batty et al., 2017). This research seeks to explore some of the challenges women face when seeking to breastfeed in this climate.

From the perspective of policy, this study brings into focus a set of experiences of women engaging in an activity the UK government actively promotes. Increasing breastfeeding rates has played a key role in the British government's goal of improving public health and decreasing health inequalities in light of breast milk's myriad health benefits to both mother and child.[10] As noted in the previous chapter, meta-analyses have consistently shown that breastfeeding reduces the risk of gastroenteritis, respiratory tract infections, asthma and obesity, with further evidence suggesting additional health benefits in terms of reducing the risk of type 1 and type 2 diabetes, childhood leukaemia and sudden infant death syndrome (cot death) (Horta et al., 2007; Chung et al., 2007).

The UK has had some of the lowest rates of breastfeeding in the world for the past fifty years (McAndrew et al., 2012). While breastfeeding initiation rates have risen in recent years due to an array of policy initiatives, duration rates still remain far below targets. Although the NHS recommends exclusive breastfeeding for the first six months of life, most UK mothers stop breast-feeding within four weeks post-birth.[11] As of 2005 only about 25% of mothers were still breastfeeding at six months and less than 1% met the policy target of exclusive breastfeeding for this length of time.[12] Indeed, over the past twenty years, six-month duration rates have only risen by a mere 2%, despite myriad public health campaigns and the extension of statutory maternity leave to fifty-two weeks (with an average of thirty-two weeks taken) (Boseley, 2011). These rates put the UK behind countries with roughly comparable maternity leave (including Canada, Australia and New Zealand) and even behind the US, which provides no paid leave at all (La Leche League, 2003) (figure 4.1).[13]

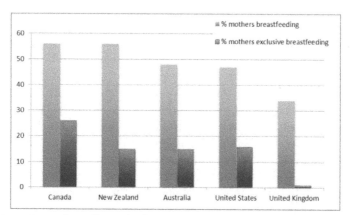

Figure 4.1. **A snapshot of breastfeeding duration rates six months post-birth in international perspective. Data from Statistics Canada Health at a Glance Breastfeeding Trends in Canada data (2010); Royal New Zealand Plunket Society Breastfeeding data (2009); Australian Breastfeeding Association Breastfeeding Rates (2010); US Centers for Disease Control Breastfeeding Report Card (2012); UNICEF-UK Baby Friendly Initiative (2010).**

In other words, although UK women take significantly longer maternity leaves than US women, they stop breastfeeding sooner. As well, far fewer of them breastfeed exclusively as compared with their counterparts in other countries. Given how low UK duration rates are compared to other countries with similar maternity allowances (and even compared to countries with significantly *worse* maternity benefits), it is important to explore the socio-spatial dynamics of why UK rates are so low. Why do most UK women stop breastfeeding before mothers in other countries in comparison? Why do so few breastfeed exclusively, and why do so many report stopping before they want to?

This research suggests that experiences breastfeeding in public may be a factor. Breastfeeding in public relates to duration rates, since in addition to access to physical, emotional and familial support, breastfeeding over time is bound up with women's ability to integrate this activity with their preferred ways of engaging with the world post-birth. Both breastfeeding and attitudes about breastfeeding in public are powerfully shaped by class, education, age, race and ethnicity (Li et al., 2005; Spencer, 2008; Tarrant and Kearney, 2008). Patterns of infant feeding can be shaped by the availability of support, the presence of an unrelated male lodger in the home, the need to be fully sexually available to a male partner on whom one is financially reliant, fear about social stigma, the presence or absence of friends or family members with experience in breastfeeding and whether or not one encounters physical problems such as blocked ducts or mastitis (as discussed in chapter 3) (Mathers et al., 2008; Pain et al., 2001). These factors all shape how easy or hard it may be for a mother to breastfeed.

Differences in breastfeeding rates also exist across different demographic groups. According to the 2010 Infant Feeding Survey, mothers identifying as 'black and ethnic minority', 'Asian' and 'mixed (ethnic) background' are more likely than those who identify as 'white British' to still be breastfeeding at six weeks post-birth, even though levels of social deprivation are higher among non-white groups in the UK (McAndrew et al., 2012: 205). For context, 86% of the population in England and Wales identifies as 'white British', 8% as 'Asian', 3% as Black, African, Caribbean or Black British, 2% as mixed ethnicity and 1% not identifying with any of the above categories (National Archives, 2012). In addition to ethnicity, rates of breastfeeding are shaped by intersecting factors of class and age, with rates being lowest among native-born white British mothers, younger mothers and mothers with lower levels of educational attainment. They are highest among immigrant mothers and Roma travellers, as well as among older mothers and mothers with more formal education (McAndrew et al., 2012: 205).

Related to the above-mentioned factors, significant regional variation also exists in rates of breastfeeding across the UK, with England and Scotland having higher rates than Northern Ireland and Wales, and London and the South of England having higher rates than the Midlands and the North (McAndrew et al., 2012). Cities typically have higher rates than rural areas, and there is also emerging evidence of significant intraurban differences in breastfeeding that map on to class and ethnicity.[14] Nevertheless, difficulties relating to breastfeeding in public can beset anyone. Indeed such issues may be even more problematic for women who have less social and economic power or who live in areas where breastfeeding is not the norm.[15] Thus as it currently stands, the achievement of policy goals relating to breastfeeding duration is down to the work of individual women and their ability to manage particular kinds of spatial performances in public (and private) space, across a wide range of social contexts and widely varying levels of social and professional support.

Breastfeeding scholarship has called attention to a wide range of reasons behind the unease with breastfeeding in Western culture. Chief among these are breast milk's suspect status as a potentially contaminating fluid that has transgressed the body boundary (Boyer, 2010; Hausman, 2003; Longhurst, 2008) and cultural anxieties about women's breasts functioning in modes other than at the service of male sexual desire (Bartlett, 2005; Hausman, 2003; Smyth, 2008; Stearns, 1999). Scholarship notes the pressure women feel to be 'discreet' when breastfeeding (especially outside the home) (Dowling et al., 2012; Leeming et al., 2013; Pain et al., 2001; Sheeshka et al., 2001; Stearns, 1999) and highlights the notion that public spaces are often considered the most unacceptable/'least safe' places to breastfeed (Dowling et al., 2012; Leeming et al., 2013; Pain et al., 2001; Scott and Mostyn, 2003; Stewart-Knox et al., 2003). Research from Australia and the US has drawn attention to legal actions and protests occurring in response to breastfeeding women being asked to leave different kinds of establishments and public spaces (Bartlett, 2002; Carpenter, 2006), and this will be discussed in the next chapter.

In addition to scholarship examining experiences of breastfeeding in public in cultural contexts beyond the UK in the late 1990s and early 2000s (Scott and Mostyn, 2003; Sheeshka et al., 2001; Stearns, 1999), a small body of research (beyond that represented here) exists on breastfeeding as a spatial experience in the UK. Leeming et al.'s 2013 study examined the experiences of twenty-two new mothers in the Midlands, finding women feeling sensitive to (and apprehensive about) the feelings of others when breastfeeding and appreciative of familial support. Relatedly, in Scott and Mostyn's 2003 study on the breastfeeding experiences of low-income women in Glasgow drawing on focus-group interviews with members of a breastfeeding support group, the authors found that accomplishing breastfeeding in this social context demanded high levels of both commitment and willingness to engage in what was perceived as counternormative behaviour (Scott and Mostyn, 2003). Participants in this study rarely breastfed in public and reported working very hard to avoid doing so.

Within the geography scholarship, Pain et al. (2001) have explored how infant-feeding choices in North East England relate to ideologies about good parenting. They highlight the broader social and cultural factors that can impact upon what are often cast as personal decisions of whether and for how long to breastfeed and how the need to find 'appropriate' spaces to feed structured the lives of women in their sample. Echoing Scott and Mostyn, few mothers in this study ever breastfed in public (only one respondent discussed having done it), so those experiences do not form a central aspect of that study. Mahon-Daly and Andrews (2002) investigated the ways in which breastfeeding can serve to mark a transition between life stages and argued that breastfeeding is structured by spatial rituals that position this activity as liminal. While that study considered issues of embarrassment and, in particular, difficulties in breastfeeding in front of male family members *inside* the home and within postnatal support groups, it did not consider experiences of breastfeeding in public space outside the home.

While these studies have made excellent contributions towards understanding breastfeeding as a social experience, a number of important gaps in knowledge remain. This chapter makes two unique contributions to existing literature. First, by analysing breastfeeding as an affective experience, it extends conceptual literature on spatial practice and urban subjectivity. And second, it provides an innovative analysis of the way breastfeeding is provisioned for in the built environment from the perspective of the social (and specifically gender) politics of design (Fenster, 1999; Greed, 1994; Layne et al., 2010; Rothschild, 1999).[16]

THE STUDY

This chapter is based on the analysis of three data sources. These include a *survey* of forty-six new mothers attending a public sale of secondhand baby clothes in Southampton (Hampshire) sponsored by the NCT in October 2008, *interviews* with eleven new mothers of first children between 2008 and 2009 (also in Southampton) and *analysis of a patent application* for a 'pod' in which mothers can breastfeed in public without being seen.[17] The size of the interview set was modelled on that of Pain et al. (2001), who interviewed eleven first-time mothers. Both the survey and interviews asked participants to reflect on different aspects of their experiences breastfeeding in public. I employed an interview schedule and also allowed for expansion and redirection of questioning in response to incoming information from interviewees (Gatrell, 2007).

In addition to this I consider the text of a patent application for a 'PLM' – a small cabin-like space for breastfeeding – made to the US Patent Office in 2009. I chose to include a US patent in the analysis both because similar data are not available for the UK and because public cultures in the two countries are broadly similar. This approach follows that of Adam Eldridge, who drew on work of a US conceptual artist to analyse constructions of 'uncivil' behaviour in public space in the UK (Eldridge, 2010). I approached these data from an defractive framework (Lenz-Taguchi, 2012), simultaneously using subjects' understandings of their own experiences as a way to understand broader cultural phenomena and recognising that my own understanding of the world both shaped and was shaped by the research encounter. Data were analysed by identifying cross-cutting themes which were then coded and interpreted through reference to the relevant empirical and conceptual literature. Interview, survey and talkboard data have been anonymised to protect privacy.

The nearly new sale from which survey participants were drawn was chosen because it served as a city-wide magnet for new mothers, attracting an estimated 300 people. This event was also selected as a way to find women who were likely to have recent experience breastfeeding since the NCT provides support services for breastfeeding women (although the annual event is open to the general public and widely advertised). It was held in a church in the in-town neighbourhood of Bevois/Highfield of Southampton, a middle-class neighbourhood bordering the university and containing a mix of middle-income apartment complexes, middle-class single-family homes and student rentals. Women were approached randomly from the long entry queue and completed the survey while they waited to enter and as they left. All but one of the forty-six survey participants had had some experience of breastfeeding and thirty-seven had breastfed in public at least once.

The interview set was drawn from a mum's group formed from a series of free parenting classes held at a local doctors' surgery (neighbourhood health clinic) in the mixed-income neighbourhood of Freemantle in Southampton in 2009.[18] At the time of the study Freemantle was a Sure Start gateway community which meant it qualified for certain means-tested government programmes aimed at new parents. Participants were all first-time mothers between twenty-six and thirty-nine years old, and their babies were between eleven and twelve months old at the time of being interviewed. All were white, British-born and heterosexual. As a new mother myself, I also participated in the group as a participant-observer attending meetings every two or three weeks in parks, cafés and group members' homes over the course of the year. All members of this group had breastfed for at least two and a half weeks, and all but one had stopped by one year. All but one member of the group participated in the interviews (the last was experiencing health problems at the time). Interviews were held in respondents' homes (or in one case in a café) and were professionally transcribed. Being a new mother myself at the time of the interviews, I shared with the interviewees a common base of experience (including experiences of breastfeeding). This likely served to increase trust and also was a fundamental factor in shaping the kinds of questions I asked.

At the time the data were collected, the in-town neighbourhood of Freemantle had broadly similar levels of social deprivation as England as a whole and higher levels than in the Southeast.[19] It had a section of middle-class housing and also served as an important receiving neighbourhood for Polish immigrants as well as containing a large high-rise public housing estate. At the time of the interviews its high street was characterised by a number of large car dealerships, a large constabulary, small independent grocers and pubs, off-track betting sites, a smattering of hard-drinking pubs and markets catering to Polish immigrants. It did not have any 'couch-style coffee shops' that can provide conducive environments in which to breastfeed. Yet despite the broader socio-economic mix within the broader neighbourhood, it is important to note that women interviewed for this study represent the more affluent segment of this neighbourhood. Most owned their own homes, all but one were in stable relationships and most had attended university. They all felt comfortable breastfeeding in most parts of their own homes most of the time. Household incomes varied across the group, and occupations of respondents and their partners ranged from engineering, teaching, supply/substitute teaching and lecturing to illustrating, sales accountancy and grounds foreman. All respondents were back at work either full- or part-time at the time of the interviews, and, perhaps reflecting the timing of the interviews with the recession, one-third of the male partners had experienced job loss within the past year. To preserve anonymity all names have been changed.

Although all members of the parenting classes were invited to join the mums group, some may have needed to return to work less than five months post-birth, lacked easy access to e-mail or space at home in which to host social events or simply already had adequate support in the form of local family (as most members of the group did not). These factors may have shaped the race profile and likely shaped the class profile of the mums group. It is also possible that potential members did not feel comfortable in a group that was largely white, heterosexual and partnered. So, although the women interviewed for this project share characteristics with many UK women who are *breastfeeding* in terms of age and education level, it does not represent the experiences of all (or even most) first-time mothers in the UK. Instead it constitutes a smaller, more privileged subset thereof. This limitation needs to be borne in mind when considering the extendibility of these findings.

BREASTFEEDING OUTSIDE THE HOME: SPACE, AFFECT AND THE MAINTENANCE OF PUBLIC COMFORT

In this first of two sections on findings I analyse women's experiences breastfeeding in public in the UK, drawing on the figure of the killjoy and the (gendered) work of maintaining public comfort as advanced by Sara Ahmed. It is important to note that data collected for this study suggest a variegated picture of women's experiences breastfeeding in public. For some this activity was not a problem, and just over half of the interview and survey respondents queried did not report any negative experiences breastfeeding in public in the early twenty-first-century UK. As one interviewee put it, 'I was more pleasantly surprised by the number of people that come up to you saying "oh isn't your baby lovely" than any kind of negative feeling about breastfeeding' (Rhiannon, breastfed eight and a half months). These comments suggest an openness to breastfeeding that is congruent with the higher-than-average levels of breastfeeding found among the middle-class women who largely constituted this sample as compared to national averages and suggest how for some the pleasure of public reactions to one's baby outweighed any downsides of breastfeeding outside the home.

This view also aligns with the characterisation of breastfeeding in public put forward within the NHS's online breastfeeding guide. In addition to practical suggestions and a statement about the simple legality of breastfeeding in public in the UK, the online guide informs potential breastfeeders that 'as you get more used to doing it, you're likely to feel more confident about breastfeeding in front of other people when you're out and about'.[20] The website also showcases two testimonials. In the first a mother observes that after she mastered how to attach her baby easily without looking, she 'soon felt confident feeding almost anywhere', reporting that she 'never had any negative comments from other people' and indeed 'didn't think people realise(d) that (she was) feeding a baby most of the time'. In a second testimonial a mother of twins avers that 'I became so confident that I hardly noticed that I was feeding them'.[21] Though providing a link to a different website presenting a wider range of experiences (healthtalk.org), I suggest that this text sets up an expectation that breastfeeding in public will be an effortless and confidence-enhancing activity for mothers who have mastered the requisite biotechnical skills.

Yet this research found a broader, less wholly positive range of experiences than suggested by the breastfeeding guide, with 49% of the study interview and survey participants reporting some kind of negative experience breastfeeding in public. This echoes a 2009 survey of 1,236 readers of *Mother and Baby Magazine* conducted by the leading UK parenting charity NCT in which

54% of respondents had been asked to leave a restaurant, café or coffee shop for breastfeeding in public.[22] The forms of social opprobrium for breastfeeding in public uncovered in this research ranged from gestures and odd looks to a looser, more visceral sense or feeling about the discomfort of others.

In the realm of the gestural and the visual, one survey respondent noted that she had 'been the object of pointed "tuts" and comments', while another recalled 'an experience of a mother and daughter glaring at me when I was breastfeeding in McDonalds'. Three more survey respondents indicated that they had received 'funny looks' while breastfeeding outside the home, and one interviewee reported that 'there was one lady (who was) completely disgusted with what I was doing, giving me filthy looks, evils' (Terry, breastfed three months). These comments suggest a markedly different tenor of experience than those highlighted in the NHS's breastfeeding guide, in which maternal confidence and competence lead to positive experiences breastfeeding in public. They speak to the breastfeeding body's 'uneasy' location at the nexus of binarised concepts of nature and culture (Grosz, 1994) with the capacity to do things that startle and shock, and highlight the way identity-based power relations can shape and differentiate corporeal practice in the urban realm. They further suggest something of the toll that can be extracted on those whose bodies are judged to be 'too natural' for the public realm (Longhurst, 2001). Relating this back to policy, these comments also highlight a serious limitation in legal forms designed to promote breastfeeding in public. Although Britain passed legislation in 2010 making it illegal to ask anyone breastfeeding from leaving a public space (the Equality Bill), none of the expressions of disapproval discussed here would have been prohibited by this bill.[23]

I suggest that these expressions of disapproval can be understood through Ahmed's conceptual work on public comfort and the figure of the killjoy. Developed as a way to analyse how racialised bodies are 'made strange' in the public realm, public comfort is defined broadly as a feeling of harmony within the majority. Relating this to corporeal practice, a loss of public comfort occurs when members of the majority are made uncomfortable by the presence of bodies understood as materially different to their own. As Ahmed observes, 'Maintaining public comfort requires certain bodies "go along with it". To refuse the place in which you are placed, is to be seen as causing trouble, as making others uncomfortable' (Ahmed, 2010: 584). To be the one disrupting public comfort is to be a killjoy: one who disrupts the comfort of others.

In this formulation, tuts, glares and funny looks serve as indicators that women breastfeeding in public are 'failing' in their duty to maintain public comfort because they are, after Ahmed, refusing to breastfeed in the normalised way, in the prescribed space. That breastfeeding should be considered as 'not belonging' in space outside the home can be understood through two of the foundational schemas of patriarchy: first, that care-work belongs in the space of the home (where it should be done by women) and second, that women's bodies function principally for the fulfilment of male sexual desire such that women's breasts are always already sexualised and that their display for any reason is vulgar.[24]

If disciplining gazes can mark a destabilisation of public comfort, so can a sense or feeling about the feelings of others. This research uncovered various instances in which a loss of public comfort was sensed rather than seen. This appeared in survey responses such as 'makes people feel funny'; 'I don't think others are comfortable with it, which made me feel a bit uncomfortable'; and 'others don't know where to look'. One interviewee commented, 'The people who see you doing it feel more awkward than you do' (Rhiannon, breastfed eight and half months), while another added that 'you could just tell that everyone else was really embarrassed and that made it really difficult . . . it was just a feeling' (Emma, breastfed three and a half months). One survey respondent noted simply that 'people accept it grudgingly'. As a final example in this stream, Emma, who breastfed three and a half months, indicated:

> I thought I'd be absolutely fine. . . . I thought I'd just get on with it and it would be easy really . . . (but) people were really shocked by the fact that you're breastfeeding in public. I kind of felt like I didn't care, but I *did* care a lot, and it was really difficult. . . . I just found it really stressful, really embarrassing, really horrible.

I would like to make two points about these comments. First, they convey how urban embodiment is an intersubjective affective experience, in which one's own feelings are shaped by those around us. As Ahmed has observed, emotion is 'what moves us . . . that which holds us in a place' (Ahmed, 2004: 27). While emotions can create feelings of connection and belonging, as the aforementioned quote suggests, more-than-visual practices can also generate a sense of being 'in the way' or *not* belonging. In this way we can see how the 'felt feelings of others' can shape women's experiences of breastfeeding outside the home. Second, in addition to highlighting concerns about the feelings of others, they raise a concern about 'not feeling what one is supposed to feel' while breastfeeding. As Ahmed notes, the sense that one's feelings are 'wrong' can lead to a sense of alienation and disrupted sense of belonging. According to Ahmed:

> We cannot always close the gap between how we feel and how we think we should feel. To feel the gap might be to feel a sense of disappointment. Such disappointment can also involve an anxious narrative of self-doubt (why am I not made happy by this. What is wrong with me?) . . . we become strangers or *affect aliens* in such moments. (Ahmed, 2010: 581; emphasis added)

Expectations about breastfeeding are set in the popular imagination through narratives about 'the naturalness of nursing' which suggest to some that breastfeeding should be easy or intuitive. These messages are reinforced to some degree to expectant mothers through materials such as the above-quoted NHS breastfeeding guide.

Like Emma (quoted earlier) who thought she would be 'absolutely fine', various study participants made mention of the fact that breastfeeding was not always (or ever) what they expected it to be. Though difficult experiences which deviated from expectations about breastfeeding's ease and naturalness, women such as Emma 'become strangers to themselves', or, in Ahmed's parlance, become affect aliens.

This section has focused on how intersubjective affective experiences – the sense of shock, disgust or embarrassment of others – can mark the limits to belonging in public space for new mothers seeking to breastfeed outside the home. In the final section of this chapter, I will extend this argument to examine how the manner in which breastfeeding is provisioned-for within the built environment colludes with this process.

BREASTFEEDING, BUILT FORM
AND LACTATION ROOMS

One solution that has emerged as a way to manage breastfeeding in public in the UK and elsewhere has been the establishment of lactation rooms: either rooms devoted to breastfeeding or a combined space for breastfeeding and baby-changing. Twenty-three of the thirty-seven survey respondents queried for this research who had breastfed in public had used a lactation room, as had all but one of the interview group. At the time of this study lactation rooms could be found in Southampton in the major downtown department and grocery stores, as well as in a major downtown pharmacy and a parent and baby big-box store.[25] Feelings about and experiences of lactation rooms varied across the study sample. Several interviewees indicated that they had had positive experiences in at least one of the lactation rooms they had used. As Shannah commented, 'The lactation room in (a downtown department store) . . . is lovely. . . . I mean everyone used it. It was the place you went to if you knew you had to feed the baby and you could get there' (Shannah, breastfed seven months). Similarly, a survey respondent noted that 'early in feeding when we were both getting the hang of it, it was good to be able to go somewhere separate'.

Meanwhile other study participants were less sanguine about their experiences with such facilities. Some survey participants noted the desire to not feel isolated while breastfeeding as a strike against lactation rooms, as expressed in such comments as 'I prefer to feed with my family rather than shut myself away' and by the comment that lactation rooms made another participant 'feel cut off from what's going on'. Others objected to lactation rooms' poor design, including lack of air conditioning and unpleasant odours if co-located with changing facilities (as is often the case). As one interviewee noted, 'At (one lactation room) the air conditioning was never working, and, like, you just used to sit there and sweat in there in the plastic seats, and it was always horrible' (Nikky, breastfed seven and a half months). A further survey respondent noted that lactation rooms often 'can be smelly and cramped or (have) chairs with arms unsuitable for feeding'. Chairs which actually got in the way of breastfeeding were noted alongside other concerns by one interviewee: 'It was just ridiculous, the breastfeeding room. The chairs were chairs with armrests, so the baby was too long to fit within the armrests (well when he got bigger anyway and when he wriggled). There were no windows in it and it's really small . . . it was like being in the cupboard' (Jenny, breastfed one year). In addition to echoing the argument advanced in chapter 2 about the ways built form is not designed to accommodate care-work, experiences such as these raise the question of whether the comfort of breastfeeding women (or babies) was the sole objective in these spaces' designs. If we allow for the possibility that it is not, what might other objectives then be?

To consider lactation rooms as a space and as an idea, I would like to refer to a patent application registered with the US Patent Office in 2009 for a 'portable lactation module' (PLM), designed by Mary Carmen Delgado-Vazquez and William Diaz-Lopez. Though registered in the US, I suggest that the text of this patent application provides a valuable means of getting at the cultural logic behind lactation rooms generally, and that this logic is broadly transferable to the UK case.[26] The PLM is a small, mostly opaque enclosure intended to create a private space in public for both breastfeeding and diaper (nappy) changing. The module includes a bench and changing table, lockable door, external docking station for a pushchair/stroller, ventilation system and window made of one-way or frosted glass (Figure 4.1). The PLM's designers emphasise the structure's small size and unobtrusive nature. They claim that 'the width need not be too much so that the module does not occupy too much space within the shopping mall or other building in which the module is placed' (ibid.), thus assuring potential customers that as little space as possible will be diverted away from shopping and consumption.

In terms of laying out the rationale for this unit, the patent notes that the PLM will serve to protect women breastfeeding in public 'from hostile people who object to their actions'. It goes on to explain that the unit seeks to remedy the problem of breastfeeding women 'being stared at, criticized and at times requested to leave the premises, therefore unable to breastfeed in a relaxed environment' by providing a space in which to breastfeed 'in privacy and in

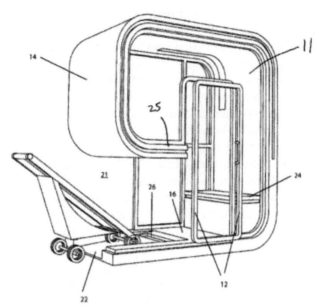

Ilustration 4.1. Portable lactation module. Credit: Delgado-Vazquez, M. and Diaz-Lopez, W. (2009). US Patent Application Number 2009/02771010 A1, Publication date 12 November, US Patent and Trademark Office, http://www.uspto.gov. Accessed 12/8/2010.

safety from the public' (ibid.). Indeed the importance accorded to the degree of isolation from the public that the PLM provides is conveyed elsewhere in the text of the patent, in a passage explaining how this unit fills a need that is not met by public restrooms (toilets): 'The public restroom is typically a distance away, and is not a totally private environment for the mother to breastfeed' (ibid.). By casting the PLM as a response to the problem of public toilets being insufficiently *private* rather than insufficiently *hygienic* conveys the impression that the former of these concerns trumps the later.

As scholarship on feminist design has argued, artefacts and socio-technical systems play an important role in shaping social relations and spatial practice (Greed, 1994; Layne et al., 2010; Rothschild, 1999). Just as the placement of baby-changing tables in public toilets (in women's, men's or a gender-neutral 'family room') can shape understandings about how that form of care-work should happen (Gorenstein, 2010),[27] lactation rooms transmit messages about how and where breastfeeding should – and should not – occur. In the description of the PLM we see a vision of breastfeeding in public in which lactation rooms offer protection from a hostile public that breastfeeding women themselves are de facto defined as being outside of. It suggests a world in which breastfeeding women require isolation, not only from unknown others but also from friends and family.

From a design perspective, the PLM would seem to replicate some of the issues noted as problems by participants in this study with regard to smell and physical layout, as well as raising new issues in terms of what to do with an older child or children in tow. Research suggests that at least some women want *some* kind of provisioning for breastfeeding in public, with research from the US suggesting that support for lactation rooms is especially strong among groups that have some of the lowest rates of breastfeeding, including African American women; young, low-income women; and those with low levels of educational attainment (Li et al., 2005). Recognising that at least some women do want some kind of provisioning to feel comfortable breast-feeding outside the home, what are we to make of lactation rooms as they are currently designed? Clearly there are issues with comfort level, odour and interior design. Alongside these issues, though, is a broader concern that by offering the means to so completely remove breastfeeding bodies from view, lactation rooms reinforce the idea that those bodies are not meant to be seen.

Sentiments questioning the appropriateness of breastfeeding in public, *not* in a lactation room, emerged in this research in comments as, 'It was nice to know that there's a place where you can go *that you are allowed to do it*' (Terry, breastfed four months; emphasis added) and from another participant who when asked whether she breastfeed in the café or the lactation room when visiting a popular downtown department store replied, 'Oh yeah, in the room. But then that's because it's there, and you kind of feel like you have to use it' (Rhiannon, breastfed eight and a half months). Connecting the *obscuring* of breastfeeding with the cultural construction of breastfeeding as an inappropriate activity in space outside home was echoed by a survey participant who observed that 'providing breastfeeding rooms re-enforces everyone's perception that it should be done in private'.

The PLM's designers position this artefact as a means of providing comfort for breastfeeding women. Relating my analysis of lactation rooms back to the argument developed in part one, I propose that these spaces can be interpreted instead as a means of maintaining *public* comfort: protecting the public from the embodied source of hostility or bad feeling. Returning to Ahmed, I sug-gest that lactation rooms can be understood in the context of a wider array of exclusionary practices deployed to maintain public comfort relating to breast-feeding in the UK. Relevant to the case at hand, Ahmed calls our attention to the Latin derivation of *dissident* as literally meaning 'one who sits apart' (Ahmed and Bonis, 2012), and in her essay 'The Politics of Good Feeling' observes pointedly that 'maintaining public comfort requires that certain bod-ies are kept out of view' (Ahmed, 2008: 7).

By offering a technical or material solution to accommodate existing atti-tudes about the unacceptability of (visible) breastfeeding outside the home, lactation rooms constitute a classic example of a technological fix; rather than helping to integrate breastfeeding into the day-to-day life of the city, lactation rooms set it farther apart: after Ahmed, they keep certain bodies out of view. In this sense, lactation rooms constitute an instance of 'designing out' certain activities (and thus certain segments of the population) from the public sphere. As feminist designers have identified the failure of cities to provide enough public toilets (Greed, 1994), and public transport systems that are inaccessible to anyone pushing a pram or in a wheelchair (Walker and Cavanagh, 1999; Weisman, 1994), as discussed in chapter 2, so have they highlighted the danger of essentialising women as users and presupposing what their needs might be. As Walker and Cavanaugh put it in speaking about the work of London-based Women's Design Service: 'When arguments are made that women use the environment differently because their daily patterns of activity are shaped by caring or domestic responsibilities, gender stereotypes of women as domestically based carers are unintentionally reproduced' (Walker and Cavanaugh, 1999: 150). In creating spaces that reinforce the idea that breastfeeding is an activity to be done out of public view, I suggest that lactation rooms inadvertently make this mistake.

Before drawing this chapter to a close, it is important to note that just as not all women encountered social opprobrium for breastfeeding in public, those who did responded to it in a range of ways. One survey respondent confided, 'The more people gave me funny looks the more I wanted to do it', and Emily, an interviewee said that 'I always had loads of phrases in my head that I would say if someone said something'. Although no one ever did 'say something', she added, 'You know, I always wanted to say "*I'm feeding my child*!!"' (in a tone of moral indignation) (Emily, breastfed two months). For some, claiming the right to breastfeed in public in the face of possible negative reactions was emboldening and empowering. I suggest that in the context of existing norms around breastfeeding in the contemporary UK, the willingness to risk disrupting public comfort can be considered as a form of everyday activism: resistance to a dominant social norm through day-to-day spatial practice.[28]

Yet for other women (even some who claimed they did not let fear of embarrassment influence their infant-feeding choice), the tension between their desire to breastfeed and the blinkered public support (or worse) was experienced as a discouragement to breastfeeding in public. As Emma put it, 'There is pressure . . . to do something that you couldn't really do in public', suggesting the tension and emotional labour involved in trying to breastfeed (as advised) on the one hand and maintaining public comfort on the other. Emily summed up the hard physical and emotional work that she found breastfeeding with the poignant reflection that stopping was like 'taking off a big coat'. These comments suggest that even for women committed to breastfeeding, the experience of integrating this activity into one's preferred ways of engaging with the outside world was hard work. They suggest something of how the accumulated anxiety, anger and uncertainty produced by experiences of breastfeeding in public can build up and ultimately leave some women feeling worn down by the sheer weight of it (even as those same experiences can produce feelings of accomplishment and pride).

CONCLUSION

This chapter has explored the role of affect and the 'comfort of strangers' (after Ahmed) in women's experiences breastfeeding in public in the early twenty-first-century UK. It extends conceptual work in geography by deepening our understanding of how affect can shape spatial practice relating to a matter of public health while extending our understanding of women's experiences of space outside the home. While it has focused on one kind of health-promoting behaviour, it is hoped that this inquiry might serve as an opening for exploring affective constraints on other kinds of health-promoting behaviours (e.g., exercise).

Breastfeeding for at least six months is recommended by health policy in the UK, yet current rates are nowhere near this goal and have changed little in recent years. While breastfeeding beyond the first few weeks post-birth delivers significant health benefits, breastfeeding outside the home (and sometimes even within it) can be difficult for some women in terms of social opprobrium. Although some places in the UK have locales that are breastfeeding-friendly, many places, like the area in which this study was based, do not. Nearly half of the participants queried in this research had had negative experiences breastfeeding in public, including experiences so negative as to factor in to their decision to stop breastfeeding.

Drawing on the work of Sara Ahmed, I have argued that breastfeeding is currently managed and disciplined in public space in the UK through affective practice, built form and expectations about the maintenance of public comfort. I have further argued that these processes are illuminated through figures of the killjoy and the affect alien. Together, these forms of emotional and corporeal management can at certain times and in certain places mark and marginalise breastfeeding women. Considering this issue through the work of Sara Ahmed illustrates how breastfeeding in public can destabilise prevailing understandings about how public space should be used. To use Ahmed's parlance, breastfeeding can be said to 'queer' public space by challenging taken-for-granted spatial practice.

I suggest that this work has two implications for health policy. The first is that women's ability to breastfeed in public plays a role in increasing duration rates. And the second is that the work of making breastfeeding in public easier is ultimately a matter of cultural change. The state can help activate such change by directing funding towards programmes that challenge unhelpful social norms relating to breastfeeding, that is, to help make breastfeeding in public less strange. Current examples of such work include third-sector initiatives such as the NCT's 'Breastfeeding Welcome Here' campaign, the Breastfeeding Manifesto's 'Access All Areas' initiative and Leeds-based 'Breastfeeding Belles', but more initiatives are being developed all the time. Finally, though beyond the scope of this chapter, significant questions remain for further inquiry, including how experiences breastfeeding in public vary across the UK and especially across areas with varying rates of social disadvantage.

NOTES

1. An earlier version of this chapter appeared in *Health and Place* (2012), 18(3): 552–560. It is reprinted here in modified form with the publisher's kind permission.

2. Though this chapter focuses on experiences breastfeeding outside the home, I would also like to flag up the many ways 'public' and 'private' in fact do not function as a neat dichotomy in practice, with home-space sometimes featuring aspects of 'publicness' and space outside the home sometimes being experienced as isolating.

3. La Leche League (2003).

4. For an alternative but related view, see Anderson (2009) for a consideration of how affective resonances or atmospheres exist in cities (but outside of individual experience).

5. On a related note, see Shakespeare and Watson (2002) for a discussion of how difference is materially and affectively experienced (not just socially constructed) in relation to disability.

6. See Horta et al. (2007) and Chung et al. (2007) for meta-analyses of breastfeeding's health benefits.

7. Health Inequalities, House of Commons Health Committee, 15 March 2009. http://www.publications.parliament.uk/pa/cm200809/cmselect/cmhealth/286/286.pdf. Accessed 15/2/2010.

8. But see Colls (2006) and Longhurst (2000) for exceptions.

9. It is not my aim to summarise this literature here but see Bell and Valentine (1995), Kobayashi and Peake (2000) and Ray and Rose (2000) for examples.

10. Health Inequalities, House of Commons Health Committee, 15 March 2009. http://www.publications.parliament.uk/pa/cm200809/cmselect/cmhealth/286/286.pdf. Accessed 15/2/2010.

11. 'Infant and Young Child Nutrition: Global Strategy on Infant and Young Child Feeding'. World Health Organization, 16 April 2002 (no author given).

12. 2005 IFS available at Unicef's 'baby friendly' initiative online. http://www.babyfriendly.org.uk. Accessed 1/6/2010.

13. Mothers in the UK are entitled to fifty-two weeks maternity leave. Employed mothers are entitled thirty-nine weeks statutory maternity pay, defined as 90% of one's wages for the first six weeks post-birth and £138 a week for the next thirty-three weeks. The government currently provides two weeks of paid paternity leave

(in addition to maternity leave) and an additional twenty-six weeks of 'additional paternity leave' if the mother or coadopter returns to work. Like maternity leave, additional paternity leave is remunerated at £138 a week.

14. Personal correspondence with David Thomas, Senior Public Health Intelligence Unit, Bristol City Council, Office of the Director of Public Health (2/2015).

15. A vivid example of this kind of stigmatisation is to be found in a BBC Three documentary on breastfeeding which aired in the spring of 2011. To quote a teen mum who appeared on that programme: 'If you take out your tits in public the chavs think you're a slag' (*Is Breast Best?* BBC Three, 12 April 2011).

16. Beyond simply being noted as one of the ways through which women accomplish public breastfeeding within cultures that are resistant to it (Raisler, 2000; Scott and Mostyn, 2003), to my knowledge no scholarly work has as yet examined the cultural significance of these spaces.

17. Questionnaire data were gathered with the assistance of students in GEOG 2004, Academic Year 2009 (University of Southampton) whose effort I gratefully acknowledge.

18. These interviews also form part of the empirical base of chapter 5.

19. Thirty-seven per cent of Millbrook residents aged sixteen and over are classified as belonging to social grade D or E, as compared with 33% for England as a whole and 28% for the South-east. Office of National Statistics, 2001 Census, neighbourhood statistics, approximated social grade, available online at http://www.neighbourhood.statistics.gov.uk. Accessed 11/8/2010.

20. http://www.nhs.uk/Planners/breastfeeding/Pages/breastfeeding-in-public.aspx. Consulted 7 July 2011.

21. Ibid.

22. 'Mother and Baby Survey Reveals Mothers Worries about Breastfeeding in Public' (unauthored), posted 24 July 2009. http://nctwatch.wordpress.com/2009/07/24/mother-and-baby-survey-reveals-mothers-worries-about-breastfeeding-in-public. Accessed 26/1/2018. The study also noted strong regional differences in experiences breastfeeding in public, with respondents in Scotland and London reporting the fewest negative experiences and those in the Midlands and the North of England reporting the most. The South-east did not emerge as either particularly good or particularly bad for breastfeeding in public. Thus while the experiences considered here should not be seen to stand for the whole of UK, it is reasonable to suppose that they at least fall somewhere in the middle of the spectrum.

23. For more on the limits of the Equality Bill as a measure to protect breastfeeding in public, see Evans (2010).

24. See Cresswell (1996) for a discussion of the way certain actions are considered inappropriate solely or principally because of where they occur.

25. For more on department stores as space to which white middle-class women are 'particularly entitled', see Domosh and Seager (2001).

26. Indeed given breastfeeding duration rates in the two countries, one could argue these rationales are even stronger in the UK than they are in the US.

27. See Cockburn and Ormrod (1993) for more on how understandings of gender, work and space can be 'built-in' to artefacts at the design stage.

28. This argument will be explored in more depth in chapter 5.

Chapter 5

Mothers acting back: Claiming space through lactation advocacy[1]

Like other forms of infant feeding, breastfeeding is a fundamental act of care (Leeming et al., 2013). Yet despite being the recommended way of feeding babies (as discussed in chapter 3), breastfeeding is not always easy to do. As discussed in chapters 3 and 4, in addition to biomechanical difficulties and lack of support, mothers can find it difficult to integrate breastfeeding into their day-to-day lives in the weeks and months post-birth due to the fact that breastfeeding outside the home is not common in the UK. Despite the fact that it is illegal in the UK to ask anyone to leave a public place for breastfeeding (per the Equality Act of 2010), stories of mums being shamed and asked to alter their breastfeeding practice in public (including a case which received national media attention of a breastfeeding mum who was asked to 'cover up' in the restaurant of Claridges, a five-star, luxury hotel in Mayfair, London, in 2014)[2] are a fixture within the UK media. The ongoing difficulties of breastfeeding in public in the UK have been eloquently put forth by spoken-word artist Hollie McNish in 2013 in her poem 'Embarassed' (Cook, 2016), which has now been viewed over 1 million times on YouTube[3] and in 2016 was made into a short film which has received 2.4 million views on Facebook.[4]

As argued in the previous chapter, interactions with strangers in public space can negatively shape mothers' experiences of breastfeeding and lead to the decision to switch to formula. With universal recognition of breast milk's health benefits among the health community in recent years (Rollins et al., 2016; Victora et al., 2016), there has been a rise in efforts to make breastfeeding in public more socially acceptable,[5] and this has included the work of citizen-activists in the form of lactation advocacy or ('lactivism'). This chapter considers the efforts of citizen-activists to make breastfeeding in public more socially acceptable through lactation advocacy in early twenty-first-century

UK. It is based on interviews with lactation activists, non-activist breastfeeding mothers and participant observation at two breastfeeding picnics in 2009. Building on existing scholarship, I argue that lactivism can be understood as an effort to expand the boundaries of where care-work is 'allowed' to take place, thus constituting what can be considered a form of *care-work activism*.

As noted, breastfeeding relates conceptually and empirically to a number of areas of research in contemporary human geography, including the spatial and embodied experiences of parenthood (Aitken, 1998; Holloway, 1999; Longhurst, 2008) and the relationship between citizenship and rights to public space (Davis, 1995; Fenster, 1999; Mitchell, 2003). But the two lines of scholarship to which this chapter contributes most directly are the politics of how and where care-work takes place (Boswell-Penc and Boyer, 2007; Brown, 2004; McDowell, 2009; Milligan, 2001) and the spatial practice of 'activist mothering' (Gilbert, 2001; Wekerle, 2004; Wright, 2005).

Building on Massey's foundational work on the spatial division of labour (Massey, 1984), in recent years geographers have begun to explore the changing geography of where care-work takes place, the social experiences of giving and receiving care and of course care-work's association with feminised labour and the space of the home. While a comprehensive review of this literature is beyond the scope of this chapter, some of the areas of inquiry that bear most closely on the topic at hand include the shift in healthcare provision away from institutional settings and towards the home (Brown, 2004; Milligan, 2001); the efforts (and difficulty of) combining care-work with wage labour through the use of breast pumps (Boswell-Penc and Boyer, 2007); and the physical and emotional labour required of employees providing care-work in the private sector (McDowell, 2009; Watkins, 2011).[6] This work has sought to take seriously the role of care-work in shaping social experience by highlighting the way caring practices are imbricated within – rather than isolated from – other aspects of social, political and economic life. As Michael Brown has put it, 'Caring must be reconceptualized as part of both an economic and political geography' (Brown, 2004: 69). This investigation extends that project by calling attention to – and challenging – the spatial boundaries that still exist regarding where it is considered appropriate to perform this type of care-work.

This chapter also builds on existing scholarship on social protests based on using one's identity as a mother as a standpoint around which to organise across difference. As Nancy Naples has observed, the transition to motherhood often serves as a politicising force motivating women to action (Naples, 1998). Building on this, Temma Kaplan rightly notes that this process can have implications for health-based activism as women: 'All over the globe . . . (assert) collective rights to protect their children against pollution and disease' (Kaplan, 1997: 1, quoted in Wekerle, 2004: 249).[7] Within geography activist mothering has emerged as an analytical frame in the consideration of urban social movements around issues related to securing the conditions needed for daily survival (food, housing, shelter) (Wekerle, 2004), and poor mothers' efforts to protest revanchist welfare policy in the US (Gilbert, 2001). Similar themes have also been explored through analyses of demonstrations and other actions in public and virtual space directed at ending violence against women in Mexico (Wright, 2005) and Afghanistan (Fluri, 2006). I extend this body of work by focusing on an instance of citizen-activism being directed at the right to perform a health-promoting activity in public. I argue that in cultural contexts where breastfeeding outside the home is not the norm (including but not limited to the UK), breastfeeding in public can be considered as a form of 'everyday' activism.

Empirically, this chapter builds on the still-small body of scholarship on breastfeeding in geography. Work in this domain includes Pain et al.'s (2001) investigation of how infant-feeding choices in North East England have been shaped by ideologies about appropriate parenting, Mahon-Daly and Andrews's (2002) study of how breastfeeding marks a transition between life stages, Longhurst's (2008) study of extended-term breastfeeding and Newell's (2013) work on breastfeeding assemblages. This chapter builds on the existing empirical base by exploring women's efforts to change norms around breastfeeding outside the home in the UK. The chapter is laid out according to the following structure: I will first provide a brief background to lactation advocacy taking place in broadly similar cultural contexts to the UK, drawing on examples from Canada, the US and Australia. I will then outline the methods used to explore the state of lactation advocacy in early twenty-first-century UK in this study and discuss findings by theme.

LACTATION ADVOCACY: BACKGROUND

Breastfeeding is promoted by a range of public and private actors at many scales. Transnational public health organisations such as UNICEF and WHO have long been promoting the benefits of breastfeeding, as detailed in the 'Innocenti Declaration', first signed in 1990 and reissued in 2005, which recommends exclusive breastfeeding for the first six months of life and continuing thereafter up to at least two years of age for babies everywhere.[8] In the UK the NHS promotes breastfeeding through both information and promotion campaigns to the general public, including by providing training and information for midwives and home health visitors, through the 'baby friendly' initiative designed to promote breastfeeding within maternity wards of hospitals (Malik and Cutting, 1998), and through postering and radio campaigns as Lisa Smyth has described in the case of Northern Ireland (Smyth, 2008). Breastfeeding has also been promoted for many years by a number of private charities. La Leche League, the leading breastfeeding advocacy organisation worldwide, has been running for over fifty years, while in the UK the NCT, Best Beginnings and the Breastfeeding Manifesto all advocate for the provision of better information about and support for breastfeeding.

Indeed, it is worth clarifying that the 'breast is best' message is now thoroughly saturated: in other words this is now considered common knowledge. Yet where problems occur is in lack of support to help mothers realise their wishes regarding breastfeeding. This can include support (or its lack) from family, friends, the general public and even sometimes health professionals, especially if they are – as is sadly too often the case – underresourced. Despite the widespread acceptance of breastfeeding as the optimal method of infant feeding, the myriad and pervasive problems of breastfeeding in a social context over time led UNICEF-UK in 2016 to issue a 'call to action' to draw attention to the urgent need to help UK women breastfeed longer.[9]

In this context, some breastfeeding mothers have themselves stepped up to try to affect social change as citizen-activists. Building on the idea of peer support (which is a core feature of many breastfeeding support initiatives), the work of some of this citizen activism has been of a public, action-oriented nature that arguably represents a departure from more traditional forms of breastfeeding promotion/support. This new wave of activism – termed 'lactivism' – is characterised by grassroots efforts to gather numbers of breastfeeding women together in one place to conduct mass 'nurse-ins', often targeting spaces in which nursing women have been asked to leave. Lactivism now also includes social media–based initiatives. Lactivism can be seen as emerging out of the magnitude of health messages highlighting the unique benefits of breast milk, and the rise of 'food politics' in which identity becomes linked to food choices and, like other types of early twenty-first-century social activism, by the ability to use the Internet to organise.

Since the late 1990s nurse-ins have captured media attention in the US, Australia, Canada and the UK (Bartlett, 2002; Carpenter, 2006; Harmon, 2005; Roberts, 2004). Events have been held in service-retail spaces such as restaurants, coffee shops, airline ticket counters, movie theatres and sometimes public or civic buildings (e.g., on the steps of Parliament House in Victoria, Australia, in 2000 in a show of support for legislation protecting the rights of breastfeeding women) (Bartlett, 2002). In the US nurse-ins leaped onto the national media radar in 2005 when newscaster-turned-talk show host Barbara Walters made a negative comment about breastfeeding

in public on her TV show *The View*, carried by ABC, and in response a
nurse-in of approximately 200 women was held outside ABC's New York
studios (Harmon, 2005). Nurse-ins have been held at individual Starbucks
coffee shops (Carpenter, 2006; Helderman, 2004) and at twenty Applebee's
restaurants at the same time (White, 2007) in response to women being asked
to stop nursing their babies within these establishments. These actions have
served to shine light on the fact that corporate policy cannot contravene state
laws which protect women's right to breastfeed in public, as they do in most
US states.[10]

Though most of the nurse-ins that have gained media attention have
targeted business establishments, one can also find evidence of (smaller)
actions in response to nursing mothers being asked to leave ostensibly public
spaces, such as the New York State Museum in Albany, New York, in February 2008.[11] And lactivism has of course entered the 'public-yet-private' realm
of social networking sites, with the 2008/2009 'virtual' nurse-in on Facebook,
in which upwards of 80,000 women uploaded photographs of themselves
breastfeeding in protest to the company's censorship of such images on the
grounds they violated the website's rules about obscenity (Sweney, 2008).
Facebook subsequently changed its policy to allow women to post images of
themselves breastfeeding.

Nurse-ins can be credited with pushing certain businesses to form policy
specifically welcoming breastfeeding and, potentially, with aiding efforts to
advance legislation protecting breastfeeding in public space more generally.
Some evidence even suggests that the desire to avoid a nurse-in can provide
the push for companies to make policies supporting breastfeeding; as for
example in 2003 when fast-food giant Burger King announced a corporate
policy specifically allowing breastfeeding in all parts of its restaurants the
day before a nurse-in was scheduled to take place in one of its Salt Lake City
restaurants (Arak, 2003; Carpenter, 2006). This example also suggests that
lactivism is not restricted to businesses catering to middle-class tastes and
budgets.

And while some kinds of breastfeeding activism have taken the form of
protests, others have taken the form of celebrations. In October 2001 in
Vancouver, British Columbia, for example, the Quintessence Foundation
launched what has become an annual 'breastfeeding challenge' in which
activists in different towns and cities compete to see which locale can stage
the biggest nurse-in.[12] By 2008 'breastfests' had succeeded in achieving a
7,632 baby-strong synchronous nurse-in across 300 sites in nineteen countries.[13] Indeed, nursing as competitive sport began to take on something of
a life of its own in the first decade of the twenty-first century, producing
some impressive results. A world record for synchronous breastfeeding in

one place was set in 2002 by 1,135 mothers in Berkeley, California, only to be broken in May 2006 by 3,738 women in a sports arena in Manila, Philippines.[14] In 2017 in the UK we see echoes of this form of lactation advocacy in events like the 'Big Bristol Breastfeed', organised through Facebook and held annually in one of the city's parks.

Lactivism can be understood variously. Infant-feeding choice is bound-up with broader ideas about parenting style, and in this sense breastfeeding and breastfeeding advocacy can be viewed as expressions of one's vision of one's self as a parent and as a mother. At the same time, infant feeding is shaped by education and social background in that mothers who are older, have more education, are in professional jobs and know others who have breastfed are more likely to breastfeed themselves (see chapter 4 for a longer discussion of this). Yet while one might expect these factors to also shape who is participating in lactivism, the breadth of cultural contexts in which breastfeeding advocacy occurs suggests that this activity is not limited to one social group or cultural setting.

These examples of lactivism are linked by a shared goal of claiming public space – be it physical or virtual – for breastfeeding while illustrating the extent to which breastfeeding outside the home is still considered transgressive. While nurse-ins bring women with common values together in physical space, both synchronous multisite 'breastfests' and actions taking place in Facebook and other social media platforms serve to symbolically link strangers with similar goals across distance. What may have begun as isolated events in a handful of localities is now occurring at broader and broader scales and within a greater range of cultural contexts.

Scholarly analyses of lactation advocacy have stressed the symbolic power of making breastfeeding visible. In her analysis of lactation advocacy in Australia, Alison Bartlett argues that what makes such actions so 'scandalous' is that they challenge entrenched constructions of female bodily comportment in which women's bodies (and breasts in particular) are sexualised (Bartlett, 2002). Relatedly, through the analysis of a nurse-in at a Starbucks coffee shop in the US in 2004, Faedra Carpenter views nurse-ins as a political performance of mothering (Carpenter, 2006). Building on the theme of visibility as advanced by Bartlett and Carpenter, I suggest that lactivism is also about raising the visibility of a particular form of women's labour. Reframing this point from the disciplinary perspective of geography, I suggest that the instances of lactivism reviewed here can be understood as efforts to expand the boundaries of where care-work is allowed (and challenge the taken-for-granted assumption that such activity belongs only in the space of the home) through the purposeful claiming of public space as a 'space of care' (Conradson, 2003: 508).

Having introduced the broader context in which lactation advocacy has emerged, I will now turn attention to the UK case. After briefly considering the state of breastfeeding outside the home in the UK, I will discuss my methods and findings on lactation advocacy in this cultural context, arguing that while lactation advocacy in the contemporary UK shares some traits with similarly directed activity taking place elsewhere, it may also differ from the kinds of activity discussed thus far.

BREASTFEEDING OUTSIDE THE HOME IN THE UK

As discussed in the previous chapter, the UK has some of the lowest breastfeeding initiation and duration rates in the world. While most women in the UK do try breastfeeding at the outset (approximately 75%), less than 50% are breastfeeding at all by six weeks and less than 1% breastfeed exclusively for the first six months (Bolling et al., 2006). These rates fall well below NHS and the WHO recommendations that all babies receive breast milk exclusively for the first six months of life.[15] UK duration rates were judged by the House of Commons Health Committee as 'abysmal' in their 2009 report on Health Inequalities.[16]

There are many reasons why breastfeeding rates fall so far short of public health goals in the UK. Some women experience physical problems such as cracked nipples, blocked ducts and infection, as discussed in chapter 3. Some have problems getting their baby to successfully latch-on to the breast and report experiencing difficulty in producing enough milk (Feinstein et al., 1986).[17] Still others lack information, social support or guidance or simply need to return to work before six months and do not have sufficient support in the workplace to continue breastfeeding after that time (Mahon-Daly and Andrews, 2002; Schmied and Barclay, 1999). And even for women who do not face any of these stumbling blocks, breastfeeding can be difficult as a socio-spatial experience, with only blinkered support (or even tolerance) for breastfeeding outside the home by members of the public (Dowling et al., 2012; Leeming et al., 2013) and as discussed in chapter 4. Despite being acknowledged as a healthy practice, support for breastfeeding outside of the home (and sometimes even within the home) is limited at best in the UK (Pain et al., 2001). As compared with some European countries where it is common to see women nursing in public, breastfeeding outside the home is still relatively uncommon in the UK (Dowling et al., 2012; Leeming et al., 2013; Stewart-Knox et al., 2003; Tarrant and Kearney, 2008). This is problematic because decisions about infant-feeding choice are influenced by women's perceptions about how acceptable (or not) it is to breastfeed in public (McIntyre et al., 1999). There are strong social expectations that breastfeeding in public be done in a way that is 'discreet', that is, conducted in such a way that the breast is never actually visible (Leeming et al., 2013; Bolling, 2006; Pain et al., 2001), and there can be intense social opprobrium from members of the public for breastfeeding in public even when it *is* discreet (Grant, 2016).

METHODS

Empirically this chapter is based on seventeen interviews with representatives from three groups reflecting a range of views on breastfeeding and participant-observation at two breastfeeding picnics, one in London and one in Southampton in the south-east of England. Data were collected between the spring and autumn of 2009. To gain a sense of activity taking place to promote breastfeeding in public at this time, I interviewed *two* NHS healthcare workers specialising in breastfeeding promotion based in Southampton and *four* organisers of breastfeeding picnics (lactation activists). The breastfeeding consultants and lactation activists were identified through consultation with midwives in Southampton, and in the case of the London activists, through a lactation advocacy website. To supplement this base, I also interviewed *eleven* first-time mothers in Southampton in 2008–2009 in order to gain insight into the views and experiences of breastfeeding in public among a more general, non-activist-identified population of breastfeeding women (see chapter 4 for a more detailed description of this data set and methods).[18]

Interviews took between forty minutes and one hour and twenty minutes to complete and were professionally transcribed. Interviews with the new mothers were held at the participants' homes or, in one case, a café. Interviews with lactation consultants were held at their place of work, and those with the lactation activists were held during or after the picnics. I analysed these data by identifying the themes to arise in the interviews and comparing these to themes raised within the relevant secondary literature. I interpreted the reflections on breastfeeding in public as reported in the interviews and my own experiences as a participant-observer at the two events both as a researcher and as a breastfeeding mother as a means to explore the concept of breastfeeding in public as a form of care-work activism.

FINDING I: ATTITUDES ABOUT BREASTFEEDING IN PUBLIC AND LACTATION ADVOCACY

Interviews with the 'non-advocate' new mothers consulted for this study reflect many of the themes raised in the literature. For some, the desire to 'want to do the best for their baby' overrode concern about how this activity might be viewed by others. As CL put it in her response to the question of whether she breastfed wherever she happened to be, 'Yeah, and it wasn't relevant. I didn't even care if it was appropriate in people's eyes because I just felt if my child needs feeding, she'll get fed, I don't care what anyone thinks'. Yet alongside this bravado the interviews also reveal some of the factors which can make breastfeeding in public difficult. One was the sheer infrequency that breastfeeding in public was ever seen, echoing the argument developed in the previous chapter. Three of the eleven mothers (together with one of the lactation support workers consulted) noted that in their experience it was 'rare' or 'very rare' to see women breastfeed in public. Three noted they had either friends or family members who did not approve of breastfeeding outside the home, and two said they arranged their day so as to remain close to lactation rooms. One reported that she had a friend who was virtually house-bound for the period of time she breastfed.

Another theme to emerge from the interviews was the view that there were 'correct' and 'incorrect' ways to breastfeed outside the home. Four participants noted the importance of discretion, with two praising women who had been appropriately discreet and two others chastising women (not in the group) for their *lack* of discretion. Echoing the point made by Pain et al. (2001) and Leeming et al. (2013) relating to concerns about bodily exposure and the sense that to breastfeed outside the home is to risk transgressing a social norm, CR remarked that 'if you get your boob out and expose yourself it's a little bit wrong'. Indeed BL put it even more bluntly: 'You get the eco-warrior types that are kind of like well it's my right to breastfeed in public, and I'll make a big scene of it, and I think that's a bit unnecessary'.

These comments convey some of the factors which can make breastfeeding outside the home a daunting prospect for some women, including lack of familial support or a broader cultural context in which it is normalised. They suggest the anxiety – and in some cases antipathy – that can exist towards breastfeeding in public that is not sufficiently discreet, even on the part of women who have recently breastfed in public themselves. Echoing the findings of Dowling et al. (2012) and Leeming et al. (2013), they convey the sense in which breastfeeding is a public performance that is vetted by others. These comments suggest how outside affluent neighbourhoods in London and certain other large cities, breastfeeding remains largely invisible as a form of care-work in the early twenty-first century and echo the sense in which breastfeeding is (still) understood as 'not belonging' in public space in the UK.

These remarks echo media representations which have tended to portray lactation advocacy as somehow unsuitable to the UK context. For example, in reference to a 2006 Delta Air Lines' action consisting of nurse-ins at forty airports in response to a breastfeeding woman being asked to leave an air-plane prior to take-off, the *Guardian* newspaper remarked that 'America has been swept by an *unusual* protest movement' (Pilkington, 2006), while the *Guardian*'s coverage of the Facebook protest – entitled 'Get Your Nipples Out of My Facebook' – included the comment that 'the problem with breast-feeding pictures is not that they are sexual or obscene. The problem is that these photographs are deeply personal and *aren't necessarily appropriate for public consumption*' (Mangold, 2009; emphasis added). While Mangold's comment can easily be extended to include actual breastfeeding in nonvir-tual space, together these texts convey the impression that breastfeeding is odd and inappropriate and belongs 'somewhere else'. Yet alongside cultural messages which seem to place limits on where and how it is appropriate to breastfeed has been a rise in activities which could be classed as lactivist. The next section examines two such events, approached through interviews with four lactation activists and participation-observation at the events.

FINDING II: CLAIMING SPACE THROUGH BREASTFEEDING PICNICS

In the first decade of the twenty-first century, breastfeeding picnics emerged as a means to promote breastfeeding in public in the UK. In 2008, events were held in parks in Southampton, Bournemouth, Birmingham, Durham, Oxford, Colchester, Plymouth, Cardiff and Cambridge, among other places, in celebration of breastfeeding awareness week.[19] Some of these events were coordinated at the local level by breastfeeding support groups as stand-alone activities, while others had a component of centralised or at least linked organisation. In addition to regional events, breastfeeding picnics were for a number of years held annually starting in 2007 in Parliament Square out-side of Westminster Palace in London, drawing sixty babies and mothers in the first year.[20] These events sought both to show support for breastfeeding women as well as draw attention to the need at that time for legislation pro-tecting breastfeeding in public.[21] The next year (in 2008) this objective was partially met through one aspect of the Equality Bill, proposed by Parliamen-tarian Harriet Hartman to provide protection for breastfeeding in public for babies under six months old (and in 2010 this age limit was then removed).[22] In addition to the Parliament Square picnics, a petition containing 3,500 sig-natures was created urging parliamentarians to 'make breastfeeding in public anytime and anywhere – safe (and) secure'[23] (including for babies and young children over six months old), with the accompanying argument that 'no breastfed child should be "hidden away"'.[24]

Through holding public events in which breastfeeding is specifically supported and encouraged, these events sought to change norms around how
urban space is understood. Like the 'kiss-ins' organised by gay-rights group
ACT UP in the 1980s in which gay couples kissed *en masse* in public locations, breastfeeding picnics are about rescripting an activity coded as intimate
and belonging in the space of the home as being equally appropriate in public
space. Following Longhurst (2008), breastfeeding picnics destabilise tacit
cultural expectations about how bodies should be comported in public, challenging injunctions against the presence of leaky bodies and even non-adult
bodies in city space (Valentine, 2004). As Morgan Gallagher, coorganiser of
the Parliament Square breastfeeding picnic observed, 'In numbers, there is
protection from the threat of being degraded, humiliated or abused', implic-
itly suggesting that breastfeeding in public is perceived at least by some as
risky spatial practice. However, she added that 'the way to break the taboo
is to do the taboo thing – breastfeed in public spaces, without fear' (private
communication with author).[25] Such is one of the objectives of breastfeeding
picnics.

On the question of location, it bears noting that parks and public squares
hold somewhat different associations than the spaces of consumption typically selected for the nurse-ins described earlier on. Parks often function as
family-friendly spaces and don't bring with them the expectation of spending
money. In this sense they are more inclusive than spaces of consumption like
the high-end coffee shops or airplanes noted earlier. Whereas nurse-ins held
at cafés, restaurants or airline ticket counters are arguably about fighting for
rights as consumers, those in parks and squares are instead about fighting for
rights as citizens.

The first case I would like to highlight is the Southampton breastfeeding
awareness picnic, held on 14 May 2009 to celebrate breastfeeding awareness
week and drawing roughly fifty people. The event was organised by a steer-
ing committee guided by NCT member Lucy Best who had organised similar
events since 2007. The event was held without any funding (thus making a
free venue very important) and in fact raised money for a local NHS breastfeeding support group through a raffle for donated prizes.[26] The event was
located in a large in-town park (the Common) that is composed of a number of
different types of landscapes (including three lakes, fields, woods, a children's
play area, an interpretive centre and a pub). The park is well used by many different groups, including dog walkers, joggers, people fishing, footballers and
of course parents and children. At the time of this research at least one NHS
surgery ran a free weekly pram-walk for new mothers in the park, as did one
fee-paying mother and baby fitness class. Owing to its large size and range
of features, the Common is arranged in such a way that different groups can
easily find spaces to conduct different activities without disturbing (or indeed

even being aware of) other users. At the same time, the Common is located in an affluent part of the city. While some of the bordering neighbourhoods have pockets of affordable housing, overall they are some of the most expensive areas of the city (indeed proximity to the Common is one of the reasons for these neighbourhoods' desirability). So although the Common is well used by a large number of mothers, fathers, babies and young children, this group likely hail disproportionately from some of the more affluent parts of town.

At the same time, although every park will have its own unique history, it has been argued that urban parks carry with them associations forged over time as being 'appropriate' spaces for middle-class sociability and middle-class women in particular (Schmidt, 1998), a status that has in some instances been maintained through efforts to keep other kinds of people (e.g., the homeless) out (Mitchell, 2003). Meanwhile, parks constitute 'nature' in a way which is nonthreatening and useable for leisure activities. Through choices about where to plant trees and activities such as pruning, cutting grass and maintaining paths, parks represent a vision of nature which is domesticated and civilised. In this way it could be argued that breastfeeding in a manicured public park creates a symbolic link between the 'civilized' nature of the park and breastfeeding as a natural, but nevertheless civilised activity. In a similar vein, picnics in parks represent a long-respected instance of blending spheres of activity normally kept separate, doing something out of doors that is normally done inside. Breastfeeding picnics in parks can be seen to capitalise on both of these associations, offering social legitimation for an activity whose 'naturalness' is part of what makes it problematic by linking it to other forms of domesticated nature and acceptable forms of middle-class practices that take place out of doors.

Within the park, the breastfeeding picnic was held by a stand of trees near a children's playground, at a distance to the nearest road (a limited-access dual carriageway), in a location that provided some visual (as well as physical) shelter. Although there are obvious safety reasons for locating the picnic itself away from a fast road, another dimension of this location choice was that it meant that the picnic was not highly visible to those not looking for it (although a representative from the local newspaper [*the Daily Echo*] did photograph the event). By using the physical environment to create visual shielding, the Southampton picnic was able to create a certain degree of privacy in public. Although other events were held elsewhere in town to mark breastfeeding awareness week in higher-visibility locations, including in the foyer of a large neighbourhood grocery store and a downtown department store, these events consisted of information stands only, not actual breastfeeding women and babies. In contrast, the Southampton breastfeeding picnic served principally to support and build solidarity for breastfeeding women and their families in an environment that was perceived as both safe and comfortable for participants while not being 'obtrusive' to the general public. So while high-visibility locations were employed as part of the spatial strategy of breastfeeding awareness week as target points for disseminating information about the benefits of breastfeeding to the general public, the event that included actual breastfeeding was designed to be relatively low-visibility.

While the Parliament Square picnic shared with the Southampton picnic the overall goal of celebrating and supporting breastfeeding in public, it differed in that it was intended as a much higher-visibility event by force of its location.[27] Bordering Parliament, Big Ben and Westminster Bridge and tube stop, Parliament Square is in an area which has some of the most foot traffic in all of London. Indeed, even the decision to have a picnic instead of a protest or demonstration was taken specifically as a way to hold an event in the high-visibility location of Parliament Square, as it is illegal to have a rally or protest within half a mile of Parliament.[28] So in this sense the picnic form was a strategic choice, a way of holding the event within a space of considerable symbolic and cultural power.

This decision carried with it both locational costs and behavioural rules. The general area is served by a tube system in which it is virtually impossible to avoid multiple sets of stairs, and the specific site is bounded by busy roads and crowds. All of these design elements pose significant logistical problems for people with prams and pushchairs (as discussed in chapter 2). In addition to this, organisers had to get prior police approval for the event, agreeing to abide by various behavioural codes so as to comply with stated guidelines (including the requirement that attendees were not allowed to display any home-made placards or banners). Acceptance of these downsides underscores the value placed on this particular high-visibility location. Since the picnic was intended as one of a number of efforts (including a petition and letter-writing campaign) to promote legislation protecting breastfeeding in England and Wales, the choice of location outside Parliament Square was made specifically to draw attention to this issue by putting it – literally – before the eyes of Parliamentarians. In addition to Parliament, the general public were also seen as an important audience for the picnic. As Morgan Gallaher put it:

> The whole concept of a breastfeeding picnic is to be seen to be breastfeeding normally and naturally, in public spaces. . . . The more people see breastfeeding in public spaces, the more normal it will become. The last taboo is being broken, in front of you. And when you see it being done in a socially public environment (sic) with society's 'approval', you get the message this isn't something you are allowed to interfere with. (Morgan Gallaher, coorganiser of Parliament Square breastfeeding picnics in 2008 and 2009, personal communication, 12 July 2009)

Thus the Parliament Square picnic sought to create a forum in which to make visible not only breastfeeding itself but also societal approval for this activity.

Indeed, the desire to promote breastfeeding in public in a way that was not seen as confrontational emerged in conversations with each of the four picnic organisers consulted for this research. Lucy Best, organiser of the Southampton picnic, noted that the goal was to hold an event that would promote breastfeeding in a way that was 'gentle, not radical or confrontational',[29] and Morgan Gallaher, coorganiser of the London picnic, described this event as a 'low key . . . socially enjoyable way of just being in a public space, without drama or friction'.[30] As Kirstie Clarke, organiser of the 2009 picnic in Stroud (Gloucestershire), put it: breastfeeding picnics are 'not about shocking people', going on to note that breastfeeding picnics were a different sort of activity from nurse-ins, which she suggested in the UK context might be viewed as ' "bolshy" . . . aggressive (and) deliberately provocative'.[31]

The breastfeeding picnics considered here share with nurse-ins a desire to claim public space for breastfeeding. Yet in each case this goal was approached in a way that seemed possible and safe in the UK context at that time. In contrast to the nurse-ins considered earlier, organisers made conscious choices to locate their events in spaces to which they were 'entitled' in one way or another – either by historical legacy in the case of the Southampton Common or through a more formal process of asking for and receiving permits in the case of the Westminster Picnic. Cognisant that they were challenging a social convention, picnic organisers all made clear that they did not want to elicit additional social opprobrium by acting in ways that might be viewed as 'bolshy' (i.e., pushy or confrontational). I suggest that this sensitivity to public perception even among women specifically trying to normalise breastfeeding outside the home can be taken as a measure both of the extent to which this activity is stigmatised in many parts of the UK and of the way social activism manifests differently in different cultural contexts.

CONCLUSION

Lactation advocacy constitutes an underexamined form of health activism. I have argued that a consideration of such activity advances knowledge and scholarship by providing an example of 'care-work activism'; in other words, efforts intended to challenge existing social norms around where particular kinds of care-work are and are not 'meant' to take place. I hope that the two breastfeeding picnics considered here might serve as an entry point to considering the various forms of lactation advocacy that are taking place in the contemporary UK. While reflecting varying levels of visibility within the public sphere, these events share with nurse-ins a desire to rescript spaces outside the home as appropriate locales to conduct this form of care-work. At the same time, breastfeeding picnics arguably represent a 'gentler' approach to social change than some of the forms of lactation advocacy that have occurred elsewhere, as UK lactation activists themselves suggest. Yet in the context of UK society where breastfeeding in public is still so marginalised (and 'making a scene' so frowned upon), I suggest that these actions constitute important efforts to try to change the status quo.

Finally, I suggest that the fact that citizen-activism has emerged as a way to normalise a recognised health-enhancing activity has implications for public policy. While breastfeeding *initiation* rates have been increasing in recent years in the UK due to a wide range of actions, duration rates remain far below targets. While there are many reasons why women stop breastfeeding when they do, the ability – or not – to integrate breastfeeding as a spatial practice with the rest of one's life beyond the first weeks and months of birth is an important factor in shaping infant-feeding patterns. Increasing breastfeeding duration rates in the UK (as health policymakers hope) may thus require at least two kinds of actions. The first is to find ways to change spatial norms about the acceptability of breastfeeding in public. And the second is to find ways to support women more fully in the period *after* they are in intensive contact with healthcare professionals (through pregnancy and birth when decisions about initiation are made), in order to help them develop strategies of managing breastfeeding in ways that are practical and sustainable in the context of their lives.

NOTES

1. An earlier version of this chapter appeared as Boyer, Kate. (2011). 'The Way to Break the Taboo Is to Do the Taboo Thing' breastfeeding in public and citizen-activism in the UK. *Health & Place* 17 (2): 430–437. It is reprinted here with the publisher's kind permission. Research for this chapter was made possible through a £1,300 seed grant from the Economy, Governance and Culture Research Group in the School of Geography at the University of Southampton, for which I am appreciative.

2. http://www.theguardian.com/lifeandstyle/2014/dec/02/claridges-hotel-breast-feeding-woman-cover-up. Accessed 24/1/2016.

3. https://www.youtube.com/watch?v=KiS8q_fifa0.

4. http://www.mamamia.com.au/hollie-mcnish-embarrassed/.

5. https://www.unicef.org.uk/babyfriendly/baby-friendly-resources/advocacy/call-to-action/. Accessed 19/5/2017.

6. See chapter 6 for more on this topic.

7. This is not to say fathers do not feel the same desire to protect their children from harm. However, since the lactation advocacy movement is led by mothers, I have kept this framework.

8. 'Infant and Young Child Nutrition: Global Strategy on Infant and Young Child Feeding'. World Health Organization, 16 April 2002 (no author given).

9. https://www.unicef.org.uk/babyfriendly/baby-friendly-resources/advocacy/call-to-action/. Accessed 19/5/2017.

10. National Conference of State Legislatures. http://www.ncsl.org/IssuesResearch/Health/BreastfeedingLaws/tabid/14389/Default.a spx (43. Accessed 20/7/2009.

11. http://alloveralbany.com/archive/2008/02/22/got-milk-nurse-in-at-the-nys-museum. Accessed 9/6/2009.

12. http://www.babyfriendly.ca/. Accessed 21/3/2018.

13. http://www.breastfeedingmatters.ca/html/challenge-history.html. Accessed 9/6/2009.

14. http://www.babyfriendly.ca/. Accessed 21/3/2018.

15. 'Infant and Young Child Nutrition: Global Strategy on Infant and Young Child Feeding'. World Health Organization, 16 April 2002 (no author given).

16. Health Inequalities, House of Commons Health Committee, 15 March 2009. http://www.publications.parliament.uk/pa/cm200809/cmselect/cmhealth/286/286.pdf. Accessed 15/2/2010.

17. See Amy Brown's work for an analysis of how experiences of insufficient milk can be bound up with patterns of structured feeding, which can lead to a 'cycling-down' of the responsive production of milk (Brown, 2016).

18. Participation in this group included going for walks in the park with babies, attending free or near-free soft-play at local churches, visiting with group members in their homes and attending weekly parent and baby drop-in events at which parents can have their babies weighted and speak to healthcare workers.

19. http://www.babymilkaction.org/. Accessed 12/8/2008.

20. http://www.babymilkaction.org/. Accessed 12/8/2008. Number of picnic attendees from http://one-of-those-women.blogspot.com. Accessed 5/6/2009.

21. Private communication from Morgan Gallager, 29 June 2009.

22. http://veronikarobinson.blogspot.com/2008/06/calling-all-lactivists.html aug 12. Accessed 15/8/2008.

23. http://veronikarobinson.blogspot.com/2008/07/open-letter-to-harriet-harmanon.html. Accessed 15/8/2008.

24. http://veronikarobinson.blogspot.com/2008/06/calling-all-lactivists.html. Accessed 15/8/2008.

25. Private communication with Morgan Gallagher, 29 June 2009.

26. Private communication with Lucy Best, 9 July 2009.

27. In this way the Parliament Square event shares characteristics with some of the events described by Bartlett (2002) in her work on lactation advocacy in Australia.

28. Private communication with Morgan Gallagher, 29 June 2009.

29. Private communication with Lucy Best, 9 July 2009.

30. Private communication with Morgan Gallagher, 29 June 2009.

31. Private communication with Kirstie Clarke, 12 July 2009.

Chapter 6

Combining care-work with wage-work: The changing policy landscape[1]

As scholarship has observed, there has been a rising interest in the role, or place, of care and care-work in public policy discourse over the past twenty years (Reiger, 2000; Reiger et al., 2009; Sevenhuijsen, 2003). Building on the framework I set up in chapter 5 regarding breastfeeding as a form of care-work, this chapter extends analysis to interrogate the rationalities behind state efforts to promote workplace lactation in the contemporary US. With the preceding chapters, this chapter seeks to extend knowledge about how maternal practice is conceptualised and understood. Building on work examining the role of the state in shaping understandings and experiences of maternity and working motherhood in particular (Bezanson and Luxton, 2006; Crompton, 2006; Perrons et al., 2006; Reiger, 2006), this chapter extends existing conceptual work on the logics of how wage-work and care-work are combined. Through analysis of contemporary American social policy relating to workplace lactation, I argue that both embodied maternal practice and normative understandings about working motherhood are being reshaped around the demands of neo-liberalism.

Breast pumps and the expression of breast milk have significantly reshaped understandings and experiences of maternity in a range of advanced capitalist countries in the twenty-first century.[2] While the medical benefits of expressed milk over formula have attracted significant research (Boyd et al., 2006; EL-Khuffash and Unger, 2012; Horwood et al., 2001; Lucas et al., 1994; Rasmussen and Geraghty, 2011), relatively few studies have addressed the social and cultural politics of combining lactation with wage-work (Boswell-Penc and Boyer, 2007; Fraser, forthcoming; Gatrell, 2007; Johnson et al., 2009). This chapter considers the cultural politics of workplace lactation in the early twenty-first-century US by analysing federal legislation passed in 2011 through the lens of feminist theory. While acknowledging the specificity of

US policy and parenting culture, this analysis nevertheless has international relevance in light of the increased prevalence of workplace milk expression in an international context (see Gatrell, 2007; Payne and Nichols, 2009; and Ezz El Din et al., 2004, for examples from the UK, Australia and Egypt) and the historic role of the US as a 'policy exporter', particularly in the area of women's workforce participation (Deacon, 2000; Dolowitz et al., 1999).

Expressing breast milk has become a normative aspect of maternal practice in the US, with over 77% of American mothers reporting having used breast pumps at least once (Geraghty et al., 2005). As Bernise Hausman has noted, 'Reliance on breast pumping as a way to manage waged labour . . . is transforming women's practices as breastfeeding mothers' (Hausman, 2004: 280). In 2011 the right to express breast milk at work began to be protected by federal law in the US under the 'Reasonable Break Time for Nursing Mothers' provision of the Patient Protection and Affordable Care Act, which mandated that workplaces of over fifty employees must provide lactation rooms and breaks during the workday to express milk. This chapter asks: What kind of normative conceptions of working motherhood does this legislation enable? What are we to make of these conceptions? And finally, what are the implications of codifying this kind of early working motherhood for feminist theory?

I analyse this piece of legislation from the perspective of Bernise Hausman's 2004 call for a 'feminist politics of motherhood' which includes, among other things, a call for more and better ways of combining breastfeeding with wage-work. I draw on policy texts, population statistics and a small selection of texts from popular media to develop and illustrate my argument. In addition to the most obvious work they do, breast pumps and the legislation regarding their use have both reshaped embodied practices of maternity and advanced a particular vision of how working motherhood should proceed in the contemporary US. On the one hand, recent legislation promotes a way of 'doing' early motherhood that validates care-work and extends rights for a (health-promoting) bodily practice which until 2011 had uncertain legal and social status. Yet I suggest that while being pitched as a means of promoting policy goals of enhanced infant and maternal health and well-being, 'Reasonable Break Time' is arguably not the best means of achieving these goals. Rather, I suggest that this piece of legislation promotes a way of combining wage-work and care-work that harmonises well with new economic forms but is highly extractive for working mothers, leading to what I argue can be fairly understood as a form of 'neoliberal motherhood'. I further suggest that by codifying this one solution to workplace lactation in the absence of expanded paid maternity leave or provisions for workplace breastfeeding, 'Reasonable Break Time' fails to deliver policy support for the full range of embodied maternal practices – and breastfeeding in particular – as called for by Hausman.

This chapter has two parts. I first review the relevant theoretical and empirical literature relating to breast-pump use in the context of the wage-workplace, including how the care-work–wage-work nexus is currently conceptualised within feminist theory. I then outline some of the key economic and political rationalities behind this bill, highlighting how this legislation marks a shift in normative and discursive conceptions of working motherhood and enables the combination of wage-work and care-work in a way that is not currently addressed within scholarship. Finally, I offer a critique of the approach to combining wage-work and care-work that 'Reasonable Break Time' promotes. I highlight how this legislation functions to synchronise maternal practice with new economic forms while at the same time structuring a 'politics of the possible' in which alternative ways of combining lactation with wage-work which are not now protected by law might be rendered harder to achieve.

LITERATURE REVIEW

Legislation codifying the entitlement to express milk at work in the US is situated within broader public and health policy narratives in which breast milk is recognised as the ideal food for infants 'everywhere' (e.g., in both the developed and the developing world) by the World Health Organization (WHO, 2011). The American Academy of Pediatrics recommends exclusive breastfeeding for the first six months of life and continued breastfeeding in combination with solids and other complimentary foods for the first twelve months (American Academy of Pediatrics, 2012). These recommendations are echoed by the US Centers for Disease Control.[3] While 80% of US women initiate breastfeeding, only 16% breastfeed exclusively for six months (based on 2009 births).[4] Although initiation rates represent a significant improvement over recent decades, duration rates, particularly for exclusive breastfeeding to six months, as recommended, are still significantly below targets.[5] Things are further complicated by the fact that, like in the UK, breastfeeding in the US is more common among older, better-educated white and Latina women and less common (and arguably less well supported) among other groups, particularly younger mothers, mothers with less formal education and women of colour. In this context, women's ability to combine breastfeeding with the rest of their lives in the weeks and months post-birth has become a matter of concern to health policy.

Meanwhile, feminist scholars have long conceptualised breastfeeding as an important aspect of embodied maternity (Bartlett, 2000; Blum, 1993; Hausman, 2004). Bernise Hausman situates breastfeeding within a broader 'feminist politics of motherhood' in which the practice of mothering is acknowledged as inherently political (Hausman, 2004: 275). To Hausman, a feminist politics of motherhood both recognises the deeply embodied nature of motherhood and calls for attending to the ways in which practices of mothering – including infant feeding – are not simply a matter of 'personal choice' as they are often cast but rather are enframed by wider social, economic and symbolic contexts (Hausman, 2004: 277) (as discussed also in chapter 3). Translating this politics into praxis, Hausman calls for the need for increased support for breastfeeding, including women's efforts to combine this form of care-work with the rest of their lives. I suggest that Hausman's theorisation of the politics of motherhood provides a fruitful way of conceptualising breastfeeding in the analysis laid out here.

Feminist theorisations of breastfeeding constitute a massive field, and this work has now been discussed throughout chapters 3, 4 and 5. However, it is worth highlighting here some of the key insights this scholarship has generated relating to lactation and the politics of integrating lactation with wage-work. First to note is the transgressive or subversive dimension of women's breasts functioning in modes other than at the service of male sexual desire (Bartlett, 2005; Hausman, 2003; Stearns, 1999), together with anxiety about breast milk as a substance which transgresses the body boundary (Boyer, 2010; Hausman, 2003; Longhurst, 2008). These insights draw on Elizabeth Grosz's work on the idea of corporeal 'volatility' (Grosz, 1994) in the context of the unpredictability of breastfeeding and the spectre of the female body 'out of control'. At the same time, in spite of these difficulties, feminist scholarship has also shown how a moral discourse has emerged around infant feeding in which breastfeeding has become associated with 'good' mothering (and bottle-feeding with 'bad mothering') due to the wide-ranging health benefits it provides (Johnson et al., 2012). This can create a condition whereby women feel pressure to breastfeed, and this too can be very damaging for women who do not breastfeed for whatever reason (Bartlett 2005; Blum, 1993; Hausman, 2003; Johnson et al., 2012; Stearns, 1999).

Moreover, feminist scholarship has conceptualised breastfeeding as contingent, variable and sometimes contradictory in meaning. Breastfeeding can be painful (Kelleher, 2006) and as discussed in chapter 3, it can be experienced as oppressive or rewarding (or both) (Carter, 1995; Hausman, 2003, 2004; McCarter-Spaulding, 2008) and can produce feelings of frustration and inadequacy about bodily capacities (especially the ability to make enough milk), as well as feelings of confidence and body pride (Dykes, 2005; Marshall et al., 2007). In recognition of the social, physical and psychological labour it can require, Fiona Dykes has argued for conceptualising breastfeeding itself as a form of work (Dykes, 2005), even as it can be experienced as deeply rewarding. Some analyses of breastfeeding have made observations about pumping, including the fact that pumping can serve as a means of returning to 'normal' (e.g., prebirth) activities (Dykes 2005, 2006; Galtry, 2000; Hausman, 2003), or as a means of obviating what are experienced by some as problems of breastfeeding, such as the loss of corporeal control and spatial freedom (Dykes, 2006).

A few studies have taken the social and cultural politics of milk expression specifically as their focus. This research has suggested that breast pumps contribute to the medicalisation of motherhood (Van Esterik, 1996); that feelings relating to breast expression can vary from embarrassment to empowerment; and that these feelings can play a role in decisions about whether or not to express (Johnson et al., 2012; Morse and Bottorff, 1988). Recent scholarship taking an explicitly feminist and poststructuralist orientation has critiqued pumping as a technological fix to maintaining the 'good maternal body' within extant moral discourses of infant feeding, by providing a way to manage pain associated with breastfeeding (and thus be able to continue to provide breast milk), as well as a means of avoiding social opprobrium relating to breastfeeding in public (Johnson et al., 2009) and as discussed in chapter 4.

This literature provides a useful background by laying out some of the key issues and critical observations about the politics of infant feeding, together with some of the ways that pumping fits into that. It identifies the cultural ambivalence surrounding breastfeeding relating to the sexualisation of women's breasts and discomfort with any substance that transgresses the body boundary, together with difficulties undertaking breastfeeding in public and even sometimes private space. It further shows how for some women, expressing milk provides a 'solution' to some of the problems breastfeeding can cause.

Despite the prevalence of combining lactation with wage-work (especially in the US and certain other Anglophone contexts), very few studies have analysed this directly. However, Gatrell (2007) and Boswell-Penc and Boyer (2007) constitute two exceptions. Gatrell's work, based on in-depth interviews with twenty women in professional employment in the UK between 1999 and 2002, reveals some of the difficulties in trying to combine lactation (either by breastfeeding or by pumping) with wage-work (Gatrell, 2007). This research highlights experiences of requests for flexible working (and other arrangements to combine lactation with wage-work) being denied and shows how lactating bodies can be constructed as unacceptable within the wage-workplace. In line with Dykes's argument about breastfeeding as labour (Dykes, 2005), Gatrell highlights both the physical fatigue of women seeking to combine lactation with wage-work and the affective strain of worry about bodily leakage and pressure to keep lactation hidden from view.

In a similar vein, my own work with Boswell-Penc approached workplace lactation through a concern with the ways gender relations are constructed in and through spaces and practices of wage labour, together with an appreciation for the different ways technology can mediate wage-work–care-work relations (Boswell-Penc and Boyer, 2007). Drawing on twelve interviews and seventeen questionnaires conducted in 2004–2005 in the US, this work highlighted the social, affective and practical difficulties of expressing milk at work (echoing Gatrell, 2007) and showed how the ability to combine lactation with wage-work in the first instance can be powerfully shaped by socio-economic class and access to 'space-rich' professional work environments.

In addition to the ways that workplace lactation relates to the wider field of scholarship on breastfeeding, it also relates to how wage-work and care-work are conceptualised within feminist theory. The primary framework for positing wage-work–care-work relations since the decline of the Fordist gender-contract and the family-wage since the 1970s has been the model advanced by Nancy Fraser in *Justice Interruptus: Critical Reflections on the 'Postsocialist' Condition* (Fraser, 1997).[6] Within this model Fraser avers that wage-work and care-work can relate to one another in three possible ways. In the first scenario, all adults are expected to participate fully in the wage-labour market, while care-work is largely marketised (the 'universal breadwinner' model). In the second, caregiving is valued in its own right as an activity distinct from wage labour and is supported by some form of government subsidy allowing parents (typically mothers) to care for their children themselves. Or alternatively, some workers (typically mothers) simply limit their participation in the wage-labour market after childbirth in order to participate in unpaid care-work. This model is referred to as 'care-giver parity', or alternatively the 'two track' or 'mommy-track' model, and is associated with the limitation of earnings and career position for mothers (Gatrell, 2007). Finally in the third model all workers limit their participation in the wage-labour market to some extent in order to participate in caring work (the 'universal care-giver' model). Through evaluating each of the three models against seven metrics relating to gender equity, Fraser argues that the last model (caregiver parity) holds the most potential for valuing care-work, destabilising the existing gender-coding of caring as 'women's work' and achieving work–life harmonisation.

Although each of the three models in Fraser's framework represents an ideal form, different countries can serve as rough approximations of what each model looks like on the ground. In an international comparative framework, the US reflects a universal breadwinner model as much as any nation, while the UK, with its much lower rates of full-time working among mothers (as compared with the US), provides a serviceable example of the two-track model. Whereas about 74% of mothers engaged in wage-work in the US are working full-time, only about 38% of UK mothers in wage-work are full-time (Tomlinson, 2007: 403). Alternatively, with rates of full-time labour

market engagement that are similar to those of the US, but within a context
of shorter-working hours culture and relatively long maternity and paternity leaves, Scandinavian countries arguably provide the closest real-world
approximation to the caregiver-parity model at present (Borchorst and Siim,
2002).[7] In each of these cases, we can clearly see how both working patterns
and trends in combining wage-work and care-work are powerfully shaped by
the character of the welfare state in a given country, particularly in terms of
the existence and length of paid statutory parental leave and the presence or
absence of universal health care.

This chapter extends existing scholarship in four ways. First, I extend
empirical research on workplace lactation by outlining a critique of how
practices of combining lactation with wage-work are changing normative
understandings of working motherhood, reflecting on how such practices
interact with discourses about how early motherhood should proceed. I then
offer an analysis of the cultural, political and economic rationalities behind
the way workplace lactation has recently been codified into law. I then suggest that this piece of legislation represents a wage-work–care-work relation
that is poorly represented within, or explained by, current conceptual frames.
Finally, I offer the concept of 'neoliberal motherhood' as a means to remedy
this.

Having outlined the relevant empirical and conceptual literature relating to
workplace lactation, I will now turn to consider the forms of working motherhood that the 'Reasonable Break Time' clause of the Patient Protection
Act enables. After placing this policy within a context of extant patterns of
maternal working and forms of maternal workplace supports in the US, I will
analyse how 'Reasonable Break Time' expands rights vis-à-vis workplace
lactation, reflecting on the politics of codifying the integration of wage-work
and care-work in this way. Finally, I consider how well 'Reasonable Break
Time' answers Hausman's call for a feminist politics motherhood.

RATIONALITIES BEHIND 'REASONABLE BREAK TIME'

'Reasonable Break Time' was pitched as a way to help working mothers
achieve their personal goals for infant feeding, thereby also helping achieve
public health goals relating to breastfeeding duration rates. Bearing in mind
Hausman's call to contextualise infant-feeding 'choice' within wider social,
economic and symbolic contexts which work to practically structure and
limit choice, let us now locate this legislation within the framework of mothers' workforce engagement and policy supports for working mothers in the
US. But before so doing, it is worth noting that undergirding this policy
framework is a powerful moral discourse surrounding participation in the

wage-labour market in which workforce participation is posited as a moral good and linked in the popular imagination with full rights as citizens. Within this view adults who are not engaged in wage-work (particularly women with children seeking assistance) are viewed with suspicion and vilified (such as was done so memorably in constructions of the benefit-receiving welfare 'queen' in the 1980s and 1990s) (Hays, 2004; Mink, 1998).

Within this context, married mothers have accounted for the greatest increase in total labour market participation in the postwar era (Cohany and Sok, 2007), with workforce participation rates among women with children in the US increasing from 47% to 73% between 1975 and 2000 (Bureau of Labor Statistics [BLS], 2006). In 2008, rates of workforce participation among women with children under age three were even higher than for women with no children under age eighteen (59.6% as compared to 54.3%) (BLS, 2006). And during the 2008–2010 economic recession, employment rates among women with children age zero to five decreased less sharply than for those of either men or women overall (Landivar, 2011: 23). Thus 'Reasonable Break Time' should be read within a context of moral discourses around both breastfeeding and wage-work, together with high levels of full-time working among even relatively new mothers.

Echoing discourses about work as a moral good, 'Reasonable Break Time' is also enframed by a social policy context reflecting some of the most minimal maternity entitlements in the world, and in which access to health care derives from attachment to the labour market. In contrast to every other nation in the developed world, paid maternity leave in the US is not a statutory right, and unpaid leave (of twelve weeks) is an entitlement only for those employed in workplaces of over fifty people (per the Family and Medical Leave Act of 1993). On average, two-thirds of US mothers return to work within three months of giving birth (Shabo, 2011), in contrast to the UK, for example, where the average length of maternity leave is six months (Hansard, House of Commons, 2007). Essentially, US mothers are expected to return to the wage-labour market as soon as they are physically able.

At a practical level, these factors create a structural and discursive environment which impels many women to return to work within months, weeks and sometimes even days after giving birth. Given the combination of high rates of workforce engagement for mothers of babies and young children, on the one hand, and powerful public health messages promoting breastfeeding, on the other, 'Reasonable Break Time' emerged within a broader socio-economic context in which combining lactation with wage-work through breast pumps had already become, if not normalised, practice, at least not exceptional (especially within professionalised sectors of the US labour market). Having traced out some of wider social and policy contexts enframing this legislation, let us now turn to consider what this law says about the changing relations between breastfeeding, maternal subjectivity and working motherhood in the contemporary US.

ANALYSIS

At its most basic level, the 'Reasonable Break Time' provision of the Patient Protection and Affordable Care Act legitimates the enactment of a form of bodywork and care-work in spaces of wage labour in a way that is substantially new. Indeed, just as Bartlett has argued that the symbolic combination of breastfeeding with other aspects of womanhood (e.g., sexuality) is transgressive (Bartlett, 2000), the integration of breastfeeding into the spaces and practices of wage-work likewise transgresses the traditional spatial compartmentalisation of different forms of bodywork and embodied labour and destabalises idealised conceptualisations of workers' bodies as bearing no signs of their reproductive capacities. In this sense it marks a sea change in mainstream workplace culture and practice in the US vis-à-vis normative embodied practice. Moreover, the process through which the bill became law rendered visible a wealth of information about women's personal experiences trying to pump at work, through the 1,850 letters submitted in response to the call for public comments (many of which were based on women's own experiences of pumping at work).[8] Creating a space for these narratives within the public sphere serves to symbolically illuminate a set of experiences which had been marginalised, hidden and in the main, powerfully marked by feelings of exclusion owing to gendered conceptualisations about normative corporeal workplace practice. Protecting workplace milk expression as a right marks an improvement on the previously limited framework of legal support for maternal care-work, and the US Breastfeeding Committee (which includes both maternal advocacy group MomsRising and La Leche League as members) as well as the National Partnership for Women and Families all lauded this legislation's passage as a step forward for working mothers (Shabo, 2011; Stanton, 2011).

At the same time, 'Reasonable Break Time' represents a kind of work–life integration that is not readily contained by existing models within feminist theory (and most notably Fraser's model as discussed in the previous section). In promoting (and offering legal protection for) embodied care-work within spaces of wage labour, 'Reasonable Break Time' suggests a way of blending of care-work and wage-work that does not fit easily within the universal breadwinner model (in which care-work is outsourced to the private sector), the two-track model (based on part-time work for mothers) or the caregiver parity model (based on a more gender-equitable division of care-work). Instead, I suggest that this legislation encourages the addition of care-work on top of the activities of a full-time working day, thus significantly intensifying the experience of wage labour for working mothers.

I have argued thus far that 'Reasonable Break Time' validates a form of embodied care-work in spaces of wage labour in a way that is substantially new and that it suggests a form of work–life integration which is not readily explained by extant models within feminist theory. I will now shift focus to offer a critique of this legislation from the perspective of Hausman's feminist politics of motherhood, examining the limits to the 'goods' of this legislation and querying what the implications are of codifying workplace lactation in this way for normative understandings about working motherhood.

One of the clearest limitations to 'Reasonable Break Time' is the fact that breaks are not waged, suggesting that who is able to take up this right will likely be structured by socio-economic class. Depending on how intensively a mother is lactating (which is linked to child's age, with older children typically receiving less breast milk), breaks of about twenty to forty minutes are needed every few hours throughout the workday in order to prevent engorgement and maintain milk supply.[9] This creates a situation in which mothers who take up this right are paid less than their full-time pay packet but are still working (and having to pay for childcare) for a full-time work schedule. The fact that breaks are not waged will likely delimit who is able to claim this right along economic lines in a way that excludes lower-income women, who are disproportionally women of colour in the US (DeNavas-Walt et al., 2011). Thus 'Reasonable Break Time' runs the risk of intensifying, rather than helping to redress, existing trends in breastfeeding duration rates in which African American women and lower-income women tend to breastfeed for shorter periods of time than Latina, white and higher-income women (McDowell et al., 2008).

Another limitation of this legislation is that it allows for pumping only and not breastfeeding at the breast. Within a policy context of no paid statutory maternity leave in which many mothers need to return to wage-work very quickly after childbirth, differences between breastfeeding and pumping are typically downplayed or ignored in policy documents promoting workplace lactation via pumping. Contra the scholarship highlighting psychosocial benefits of breastfeeding (as opposed to pumping) (Schmied and Lupton, 2001), within this context the myriad affective, emotional and biomechanical differences between the two practices are flattened. Instead, the benefits of breastfeeding are symbolically distilled down to, and contained within, the substance or matter of breast milk itself (Smith, 2004). Pumping is then constructed as being 'as good as' breastfeeding in terms of the nutritional and immunological benefits for the baby.

Yet just as practices of pumping and breastfeeding are different, so is breast milk nursed by a baby different from expressed milk in a bottle. While better (in terms of nutritional and immunological benefits) than formula, expressed breast milk that has been refrigerated or frozen is materially different from fresh. Breast milk is a dynamic compound that changes composition in response to time of day, immediate climatic conditions, age of child, health of mother and other factors (Hyde, 2012). The 'tailor made' aspect of breast milk is lost when frozen and given at a different time or in a different place. Even under ideal circumstances of refrigeration, the nutritional content of expressed milk begins to degrade within twenty-four hours, with significant loss of vitamins C, A and E in milk that has been refrigerated or frozen (Ezz El Din et al., 2004). For example, the nutritional value of vitamin C in expressed milk that has been refrigerated twenty-four hours reflects a 36% drop in nutritional value as compared to fresh, while milk that has been frozen one week reflects a 60% drop (Ezz El Din et al., 2004). Biological properties of milk have also shown to degrade over time through processes of refrigeration and freezing (Francis et al., 2012; Hyde, 2012).[10] This is to say that despite the desire to downplay differences between fresh and expressed breast milk that is latent in policy narratives promoting workplace lactation, material differences exist between them. These findings sit uncomfortably with workplace legislation which offers pumping as the only means of capturing the full range of immunological and health benefits associated with breastfeeding.

As well, although some women prefer pumping to nursing (Johnson et al., 2012; Morse and Bottorff, 1988), many do not, and research has outlined the personal and political difficulties of trying to combine lactation with wage-work (Boswell-Penc and Boyer, 2007; Gatrell, 2007). In fact, the years leading up to the passage of the Patient Protection and Affordable Care Act saw something of a breast pump 'backlash' in the US media, through the publication of several high-profile stories (including in the *New Yorker*, *the Atlantic* and the *New York Times*) raising concern about the shift to workplace milk-expression as a normative practice (Lapore, 2009; Rosin, 2009; Warner, 2009). While it is to be noted that these news outlets reflect a predominantly East Coast readership and cater to a wealthier, whiter segment of the American public than the population as a whole, I nevertheless suggest that they point to common frustrations among mothers who have tried to combine lactation with wage-work and common concerns over how breast pumps are reshaping normative practices of working motherhood that extend well beyond 'mother-focused' news outlets (e.g., the so-called mommy media/ mommy blogs).

Echoing the seminal work of feminist science and technology studies scholar Ruth Schwartz Cowan as outlined in her book *More Work for Mother* (Cowan, 1983), Hannah Rosin has suggested that, like so many other twentieth-century domestic appliances, breast pumps ultimately generate more labour than they save. Indeed, Rosin casts pumping as 'the moment that . . . brings together all the awfulness of being a modern mother' (Rosin, 2009: no page number available). In a similar vein, in an article titled simply 'Ban the Breast Pump', Judith Warner portrays pumping as a 'grotesque ritual', stating she:

> hope (s) that some day, not too long in the future, books on women's history will feature photos of breast pumps to illustrate what it was like back in the day when mothers were consistently given the shaft. Future generations of female college students will gaze upon the pumps, aghast. (Warner, 2009: no page number available)

In 1997 Judith Galtry first called attention to the class politics of pumping, associating breast pumps with socio-economic privilege (Galtry, 2000). By 2009 feminist commentators such as those noted previously were beginning to suggest that breast pumps may have become a 'privilege' some women didn't want. Written two years before 'Reasonable Break Time' was passed into law, each of these pieces questioned 'how good' the goods of breast pumping actually are: both because it is so labour-intensive and because it is so unlike breastfeeding.

Approaching 'Reasonable Break Time' from the perspective of Hausman's feminist politics of motherhood, I have analysed some of the wider social, economic, biomedical and symbolic contexts that shape the kind of maternal practice this legislation promotes. I have argued that 'Reasonable Break Time' is informed by political–economic logics and rationalities which reflect dual moral narratives about the beneficence of breastfeeding, on the one hand, and the good of full-time engagement in the workforce, on the other, in a policy framework of minimal maternity leave. Returning to the question structuring this discussion regarding the implications for normative conceptions of working motherhood of codifying workplace lactation in this way, I suggest that 'Reasonable Break Time' encourages combining lactation with wage-work in a way that is as labour-intensive as breastfeeding, but without any of the affective/interpersonal benefits – and indeed less of the nutritional and immunological benefits. I suggest that while this legislation represents a recognition and valuing of care-work in space of wage labour, it binds normative conceptions of working motherhood to a particularly intensive form of maternal practice. Relating back to Hausman's call for 'more and better' ways of combining lactation with wage-work, I submit that 'Reasonable Break Time' falls short in terms of creating options which are both substantially better and available equally to all working mothers.

'Reasonable Break Time' was promoted as a means to both capture the full medical benefits of breastfeeding and enhance the well-being of working mothers. I have argued here that it does not achieve either aim as well as it might. Taking as a hypothesis that expanding the field of choice relating to workplace lactation to include actual breastfeeding as well as longer, paid maternity leaves would both benefit infant and maternal health and well-being, as well as getting closer to Hausman's vision of motherhood, I pose the question: What is achieved by narrowing this field to support only pumping?

By way of drawing my analysis to a close, I suggest that while 'Reasonable Break Time' does not function as well as other solutions might for working mothers seeking to combine lactation with wage-work, it functions very well in terms of advancing broader economic rationalities of neoliberalism in the particular way that it is constituted in the contemporary US. While economic forms, approaches to the market and ways of working associated with neo-liberalism are both variable and highly culturally specific, after Diane Perrons et al. I am using this term to refer to long working hours and a high degree of integration between work and nonwork activities (Perrons et al., 2006). As Perrons et al. have observed about the way new economic regimes have reshaped gender relations in recent years: 'Macro level changes are affecting the micro-organization of daily life (including) working patterns and gender divisions in Northern and Western Europe and the United States' (Perrons et al., 2006: 2). Relatedly, considering the influence of neoliberalism on maternity policy in Australia, Kerreen Reiger has argued that states can craft policy that both satisfy broader economic demands and reflect current social concerns (Reiger, 2006). Building on this I suggest that 'Reasonable Break Time' reveals the power of extant economic regimes to shape not only gender relations but also a bodily practice as intimate as breastfeeding.

The form of work–life integration 'Reasonable Break Time' promotes is characteristic of a mode of neoliberal citizenship in which individuals are responsibilised for the maintenance of their own health and welfare (and, for mothers) of their families (Bezanson and Luxton, 2006; Rose, 1999). Under 'Reasonable Break Time', the responsibility for children's health is achieved through an almost wholly individuated socio-technical system of breast pumps, lactation rooms, refrigerators and working mothers willing to discipline their bodies to the rigours of pumping at work. This costs organisa-tions relatively little when compared with robust maternity leave, in terms of both maternity pay and lost labour. As well, pumping at work offers a way for breast milk to (eventually) get to babies in a way that is far less impactful on spaces and practices of wage labour than bringing babies into spaces of wage-work every time they needed to be fed would be. In this way, like other kinds of technologies before them, breast pumps become woven into and help support particular economic configurations and gendered ways of working (Layne et al., 2010).

In this way 'Reasonable Break Time' promotes *neoliberal mothering* by advancing a form of maternal practice that is congruent with the rigorous mode of workforce participation associated with neoliberalism while also being responsive to expectations about delivering 'the best for ones' baby', especially where infant health is concerned. In this sense combining lactation with wage-work via breast pumping fits within a style of intensive mothering associated with the Anglo-American middle class which is characterised by privileging the child's needs (or perceived needs) above other factors and shares with neoliberal citizenship a nominative zeal for identifying and neutralising potential risks to health (Fox, 2006; Hays, 1998).

Finally, after the work of Rancière (2010) and Mouffe (2005), I suggest that this legislation structures a politics of the possible, creating consensus around how working motherhood and workplace lactation should proceed in a way that makes it more difficult to argue for other ways of combining breastfeeding with wage-work (since a solution for this has now been provided). 'Reasonable Break Time' essentially establishes a new order vis-à-vis workplace lactation; and every order, as Mouffe reminds us, 'is predicated on the exclusion of other possibilities' (Mouffe, 2005: 18). Interwoven as it is with moral discourses about workforce participation and reflecting a policy context in which differences between breastfeeding and pumping are downplayed, 'Reasonable Break Time' has the potential to render calls for alternatives which would take lactating women out of the wage labour market (e.g., for longer, paid maternity leaves) appear unnecessary.[11]

CONCLUSION

This chapter has offered a theorisation of how maternal practices and conceptions of working motherhood in the US have shifted in recent decades as workplace milk expression has become more prevalent. Through an analysis of the 'Reasonable Break Time' provision of the Patient Protection and Affordable Care Act of 2011, I have shown how normative expectations of working motherhood have shifted in ways that mark a radical departure from policy supports for breastfeeding found in all other Western democracies. Although nominatively intended to advance public health goals, when looked at up-close, it appears that right-to-pump legislation supports certain kinds of working more clearly than it does policy goals relating to maternal and infant health. I have thus argued that such legislation promotes a normative ideal of 'good' early motherhood which is congruent with broader economic logics of post-Fordism (Perrons et al., 2006; Rose, 1999), but which is particularly extractive for working mothers.

Building on Layne et al. (2010), I have shown how socio-technical systems can be marshalled to provide support for particular gender and work regimes and how breast pumps in particular can serve as a means by which working mothers are responsibilised for the care of the family within the consensus view that early motherhood should include a rapid return to full-time work (e.g., within the first few months if not weeks postpartum). Without longer maternity leaves or the potential to nurse at work, I argue that the 'solution' to combining lactation with wage-work advanced by 'Reasonable Break Time' marks the ascendance of a form of maternal subjectivity which is principally shaped by and aligned to the demands of neoliberal citizenship (Bezanson and Luxton, 2006; Rose, 1999). In this sense I suggest that right-to-pump legislation advances a form of maternal practice which can be understood as 'neoliberal motherhood', in other words combining elements of intensive motherhood with a high degree of integration between wage-work and care-work. While representing an improvement on what came before in terms of policy supports for workplace lactation, 'Reasonable Break Time' ultimately fails to deliver the kind of social and policy change that would be needed to achieve Hausman's 'feminist politics of motherhood'. As ever, further work is needed in realms of theory, policy and practice in order to bring us closer to this aim.

NOTES

1. An earlier version of this chapter appeared in print under the title 'Neoliberal Motherhood: Workplace Lactation and Changing Conceptions of Working Motherhood in the Contemporary US' (2014) in the journal *Feminist Theory* 15(3): 269–288. It is reprinted here in modified form with the kind permission of the publisher.

2. I use the term 'milk expression' in a broad sense to refer to any method of getting milk out of the breast other than by a baby. I further use the terms 'pumping' and 'expressing milk' interchangeably throughout the chapter.

3. http://www.cdc.gov/breastfeeding/faq/. Accessed 16/8/2012.

4. Breastfeeding Report Card, Centers for Disease Control, 2012. http://www.cdc.gov/breastfeeding/data/reportcard.htm. Accessed 19/8/2012.

5. Though, as noted earlier, still higher than UK duration rates.

6. See Borchorst and Siim (2002); Lister (2008); Noddings (2001); Perrons (2000); and Weir (2005) for examples of engagements with this framework.

7. Though with increasing numbers of stay-at-home fathers in the US, Canada, the UK and elsewhere, new configurations are also beginning to emerge.

8. At the time of writing this information was available at: http://www.usbreastfeeding.org/p/cm/ld/fid=28 , however it has since been taken down.

9. Lactation is a dynamic process whereby the amount of milk produced is a response to the amount consumed/extracted; thus in order to keep producing milk, a lactating woman must continue to breastfeed (or express).

10. These findings are perhaps especially problematic in light of the common practice among working mothers of saving frozen milk for weeks or months as insurance against foreseen and unforeseen absences from home (e.g., out-of-town conferences or other work trips) (Payne and Nichols, 2010).

11. The fact that major women's groups did not raise concerns over this legislation can be read as evidence of the ways public discourse is constrained in the US regarding discussion over the question of workplace lactation.

Conclusion

In these chapters I have extended understanding of the spatial, embodied and material politics of early motherhood, based on primary research from the contemporary US and UK. Chapter 1 outlined some of the kinds of identity transformations that can occur to women post-birth, positing early motherhood as a kind of becoming. Through engagements with New Materialist, feminist and Deleuzian theories, I advance understanding about the role of spatial practice in projects of becoming, highlighting the importance of considering how identities or subjective self-understandings change over time. Chapter 2 explored mothers' experiences of journey-making in East London, employing concepts of mother–baby assemblages, affective environments and material entanglements to highlight some of the challenges mothers can face in becoming mobile with a small baby in a dense urban environment. Chapter 3 considered the expanded field of agency at play in breastfeeding, advancing an analysis of breast milk as an agentic force within breastfeeding assemblages based on women's experiences breastfeeding that do not go according to plan due to physical problems.

Chapter 4 examined issues relating to breastfeeding outside the home in the contemporary UK based on evidence from the south-east of England. This chapter explored the agency of strangers in mothers' experiences of breastfeeding and argued that subtle, often nonverbal expressions of disapproval from members of the public can shape experiences of breastfeeding and decisions about when to stop. In turn chapter 5 explored the activities of mothers seeking to make breastfeeding in public more common in the UK. This chapter showed how spatial norms are not written in stone but rather are changeable through social action. Finally, chapter 6 explored the changing policy landscape regarding the combination of lactation with wage-work, arguing that current US policy advances a vision of working motherhood that is both congruent with neoliberalism and particularly burdensome to new mothers.

This work advances existing scholarship in the field in a number of ways. One key contribution it makes is to explore the concept of what could be termed 'post-humanist motherhood', by which means an understanding of maternal practice which includes non-human agents (e.g., prams, built form, breast milk) within the analytical frame. Through this approach I advance an understanding of motherhood as a state of distributed agency across both human and non-human forces, including but not limited to not only parents and babies but also matter, policies, affects and even members of the public. Following on from this, I also advance scholarship on the concept of *natureculture* (i.e., the way nature and culture exist as an inextricably interconnected monism rather than a binism) through my analysis of agentic matter within the body.

Shifting to consider the contributions this book might make to policy and practice, I have advanced a conceptualisation of breastfeeding as a form of care-work and argue that we can consider the efforts of mothers (and others) to normalise breastfeeding outside the home as a form of *care-work activism*. Finally, I argue that we can understand the way US policy encourages mothers to combine lactation with wage-work as a form of *neoliberal motherhood* as a way of showing how this policy promotes public health objectives in the context of very short maternity leaves. I hope this research might be useful to scholars and students as well as those in policy and practice and that it might spur further research on these themes in fields of geography, anthropology, sociology, nursing and midwifery and the interdisciplinary fields of motherhood, infant feeding and parenting studies.

Although this book is not a comparative study as such, the research herein nevertheless flags up some of the ways motherhood is experienced in particular ways in particular places, with experiences being shaped by local and national contexts as well as intersecting systems of privilege and discrimination. For example, experiences of becoming mobile with a small baby in a very dense, urban area like London that relies heavily on public transportation (as discussed in chapter 2) will differ in important ways from mothering in contexts that are more car-dependent. Likewise, experiences of breastfeeding outside the home in social contexts where it is more normative will differ from the kinds of experiences (and struggles) discussed in chapters 4 and 5. And experiences of combining lactation with wage-work, as discussed in chapter 6, will differ by national-level policy and cultural context, as well as by the degree of social privilege possessed by a given mother. Together this work shows both the power of policy to shape women's experiences of early motherhood and the power of cultural context to shape these experiences in ways we might not expect based on policy alone.

Over the course of bringing this book together scholarship across the fields to which it contributes has continued to grow in exciting ways. This work has brought forth useful analyses of how the spaces and politics of motherhood continue to unfold. Before concluding I would like to note some of these as I believe they give an 'expanded view' in which to situate the analyses put forward here. To give the briefest sample of some of this work: Eleni Bourantani has explored fathers' evolving role in early childcare in the UK in the context of expanding paternity leave (Bourantani, forthcoming), pointing to the ways the gender of childcare and nature of parenting itself is shifting, while Carla Barrett has examined the negotiation of household work and emotional labour within LGBTQ families in the UK (Barrett, 2015). Through engagements with queer theory both scholars explore the concept of *queering* the gender order itself as it relates to parenting and other kinds of care-work as a way to think and act our way towards less-binarised understandings of bodywork, emotion-work and spatial practice in relation to parenting.

Meanwhile Holt, Waight and Dowling have highlighted the role of actors and forces other than parents within parenting assemblages: Holt by highlighting the agency of babies (Holt, 2013); Waight by exploring the role of 'baby things' and other materials that become enlisted in parenting (Waight, 2014); and Dowling through an investigation into the conceptually rich question of breast milk sharing (Dowling, forthcoming). These new and emerging trajectories all usefully extend the project of helping us recognise the power of forces beyond (adult) human actors in shaping parenting practice and as such help deepen our understanding of the politics of such practices.

Drawing on a rich base of ethnographic fieldwork with parents in the first year post-birth, Cecilia Tomori has unveiled heretofore hidden geographies of nighttime parenting practice and micro-geographies of the home (Tomori, 2014), and Fiona Giles has explored the ways mothering in the age of social media destabilises public–private binaries, from the potential to send breast-feeding selfies to the world from the privacy of a bedroom to the concept of the mother–baby breastfeeding dyad as a public unto itself (Giles, forthcoming). This vibrant body of scholarship signals the expanding interest in the spaces and politics of parenthood in the home, in public space, at work and in cyberspace, highlighting just some of the many exciting new directions work in this field is taking.

From the perspective of policy and practice, parenting and infant feeding have seen a number of changes in the UK context over the course of this book's writing. While some of these changes have been positive, there have also been many changes that have made life more challenging for UK families. While the extension of paternity leave potentially creates exciting new possibilities for more gender-mutual forms of parenting (as suggested earlier), the broader landscape of austerity budgeting since the Conservative government has been in power has meant cuts to a wide range of programmes and services and creation of new forms of tax that have made life harder for low-income and socially excluded parents in the UK (Jupp, 2017).

In addition to the bedroom tax, which has hit low-income families especially hard, in 2010 the Conservatives took away dedicated funding for Sure Start centres, facilities which offer support and care for lower-income new parents (Torjesen, 2016). Over the period of writing this book, England had no 'lead' office or person to promote breastfeeding, and Wales did away with the position of breastfeeding lead that they did have. In 2011 funding was withdrawn for breastfeeding awareness week, and after the 2010 IFS, the UK government took the decision to discontinue this most-valuable, comprehensive resource which had taken place every five years since 1975.[1]

In response to these moves, a range of advocates and policymakers have highlighted the need for renewed attention to providing more support to mothers and families in the UK. In addition to efforts to help low-income and socially disadvantaged mothers and families who have been especially hard hit by austerity, there have been a range of initiatives to bring renewed support for breastfeeding. This also feeds into a social justice agenda because, as things currently stand, fewer socially disadvantaged mothers and their babies receive the health and other benefits of breastfeeding as compared to their more-privileged counterparts. For example, in 2016 UNICEF-UK issued a 'call to action' to raise the issue of breastfeeding,[2] and Scottish National Party Parliamentarian for Glasgow Central Alison Thewliss convened an All-Party Parliamentary Group on Infant Feeding to push questions of infant feeding and inequality up the policy agenda.[3] Alongside these initiatives at the level of policy, in the realm of 'everyday activism', social media continues to take on an ever-more prominent role in initiatives pushing for increased acceptance of breastfeeding in public, such as through breast-fests, nurse-ins and the like. Through these initiatives both women's experiences of early motherhood and activism by and on behalf of new mothers will continue to change and evolve in ways that continue to warrant our attention.

Herein I have offered a – necessarily selective – analysis of the spaces and politics of early motherhood in the UK and US. Building on a venerable legacy of scholarship on motherhood, I hope to have extended knowledge relating both to theory (particularly on questions of embodiment, relationality, material agency and the more-than-human) and to more grounded concerns with the (sometimes micro-) politics of socio-spatial practice, embodied social action and everyday activism. And I would argue that *both* approaches (grounded and theoretical) are necessary in order to gain a complete understanding of what early motherhood is and means. I hope these analyses prove useful and take scholarship forward and likewise look forward to seeing how this exciting field continues to develop and evolve in response to both new innovations in feminist and socio-spatial theory and ever-changing political contexts.

NOTES

1. http://digital.nhs.uk/catalogue/PUB08694. Accessed 17/10/2017.
2. https://www.unicef.org.uk/babyfriendly/baby-friendly-resources/advocacy/call-to-action/. Accessed 22/10/2017.
3. http://www.alisonthewliss.scot/category/breastfeeding/. Accessed 22/10/2017. Thewliss and the Infant Feeding and Inequality All Party Parliamentary Group (APPG) has advanced specific initiatives to provide more support for breastfeeding mothers, make more breastfeeding-friendly places and place limits on the advertising and sale of human milk substitutes.

Bibliography

Adey, P. (2006). If mobility is everything then it is nothing: Towards a relational politics of (im) mobilities. *Mobilities* 1(1): 75–94.

Ahmed, S. (2004). Collective feelings: Or, the impressions left by others. *Theory, Culture & Society* 21(2): 25–42.

Ahmed, S. (2008). The politics of good feeling. *Australian Critical Race and Whiteness Studies Association* 4(1): 1–18.

Ahmed, S. (2010). Killing joy: Feminism and the history of happiness. *Signs* 3(35): 571–594.

Ahmed, S. and Bonis, O. (2012). Feminist killjoys (and other wilful subjects). *Cahiers du Genre* 2: 77–98.

Aitken, S. C. (1998). *Family fantasies and community space*. New Brunswick, NJ: Rutgers University Press.

Aitken, S. C. (2000). Fathering and faltering: 'Sorry but you don't have the necessary accoutrements'. *Environment and Planning A* 32(4): 581–598.

Alaimo, S. and Hekman, S. J., eds. (2008). *Material feminisms*. Bloomington, IN: Indiana University Press.

American Academy of Pediatrics. (2012). Breastfeeding and the use of human milk. *Policy Statement Pediatrics* 129(3): 827–841.

Anderson, B. (2009). Affective atmospheres. *Emotion, Space and Society* 2(2): 77–81.

Anderson, K. (2014). Mind over matter? On decentring the human in human geography. *Cultural Geographies* 21(1): 3–18.

Anderson, K. and Perrin, C. (2015). New Materialism and the stuff of humanism. *Australian Humanities Review* 58: 1–15.

Arak, J. (2003). Burger King: Breast-feeding fine. *CBS News*, 22 November [online] available at http://www.cbsnews.com/stories/2003/11/22/national/main585110.shtml (accessed 8 June 2009).

Asher, R. (2011). *Shattered: Modern motherhood and the illusion of equality*. New York, NY: Random House.

Australian Breastfeeding Association. (2010). Breastfeeding rates in Australia. Available at breastfeeding.asn.au/bf-info/general-breastfeeding-information/breastfeeding-rates-australia (accessed 2 January 2015).

Baby Friendly. (2006). Baby Friendly Newsletter. July. Available at http://www.baby-friendly.ca/(accessed 23 February 2018).

Baby Milk Action. (2008). Baby Milk Action IBFAN. Available at babymilkaction.org (accessed 12 August 2008).

Bailey, L. (1999). Refracted selves? A study of changes in self-identity in the transition to motherhood. *Sociology* 33(2): 335–352.

Barad, K. (2007). *Meeting the universe halfway: Quantum physics and the entanglement of matter and meaning*. Durham, NC and London, UK: Duke University Press.

Barad, K. (2008). Posthumanist performativity: Toward an understanding of how matter comes to matter. In Alaimo, S. and Hekman, S. (eds.), *Material feminisms*. Bloomington, IN: Indiana University Press, pp. 120–156.

Baraitser, L. (2009). *Maternal encounters: The ethics of interruption*. London, UK: Routledge.

Barrett, C. (2015). Queering the home: The domestic labour of lesbian and gay couples in contemporary England. *Home Cultures* 12(2): 193–211.

Bartlett, A. (2000). Thinking through breasts: Writing maternity. *Feminist Theory* 1(2): 173–186.

Bartlett, A. (2002) Scandalous practices and political performances: Breastfeeding in the city. *Continuum: Journal of Media and Cultural Studies* 16(1): 111–121.

Bartlett, A. (2003). Breastfeeding bodies and choice in late capitalism. *Hecate* 29(2): 153.

Bartlett, A. (2005). *Breastwork: Rethinking breastfeeding*. Sydney, Australia: University of New South Wales Press.

Bates, L. (2016). *Everyday sexism: The project that inspired a worldwide movement*. Basingstoke, UK: Macmillan.

Batty, D., Weale, S. and Bannock, C. (2017). Sexual harassment 'at epidemic levels' in UK universities. *The Guardian* [online] 5 March, available at https://www.theguardian.com/education/2017/mar/05/students-staff-uk-universities-sexual-harassment-epidemic (accessed 16 October 2017).

Bell, D. and Valentine, G. (1995). *Mapping desire: Geographies of sexualities*. London, UK: Psychology Press.

Bennett, J. (2010). A vitalist stopover on the way to a new materialism. *New Materialisms: Ontology, Agency, and Politics* 91(1): 47–69.

Bezanson, K. and Luxton, M. (2006). *Social reproduction: Feminist political economy challenges neo-liberalism*. Montreal, Canada: McGill-Queen's Press.

Bissell, D. (2009). Conceptualising differently-mobile passengers: Geographies of everyday encumbrance in the railway station. *Social & Cultural Geography* 10(2): 173–195.

Blum, L. M. (1993). Mothers, babies and breastfeeding in late capitalist America: The shifting contexts of feminist theory. *Feminist Studies* 19(3): 291–311.

Bolling, K., Grant, C., Hamlyn, B. and Thornton, A. (2007). Infant Feeding Survey 2005. Available at http://digital.nhs.uk/catalogue/PUB00619 (accessed 23 February 2018).

Borchorst, A. and Siim, B. (2002). The woman-friendly welfare states revisited. *NORA-Nordic Journal of Feminist and Gender Research* 10(2): 90–98.

Borra, C., Iacovou, M. and Sevilla, A. (2015). New evidence on breastfeeding and postpartum depression: The importance of understanding women's intentions. *Maternal and Child Health Journal* 19(4): 897–907.

Boseley, S. (2011). Breastfeeding week dropped by government. *The Guardian*, 18 June, 10.

Boswell-Penc, M. and Boyer, K. (2007). Expressing anxiety? Breast pump usage in American wage workplaces. *Gender, Place and Culture* 14(5): 151–167.

Bourantani, E. (forthcoming). *Regendering care in the UK: Experiences of male primary carers*, PhD dissertation, University of Southampton.

Bowlby, S. (1990). Women, work and the family: Control and constraints. *Geography* 76: 17–26.

Boyd, C., Quigley, M. and Brocklehurst P (2006) Donor breast milk versus infant formula for preterm infants: Systematic review and meta-analysis. *ADS Child Fetal Neonatal Edition* 92(3): 169–175.

Boyer, K. (2010). Of care and commodities: Breast milk and the politics of mobile bio-substances. *Progress in Human Geography* 34(1): 5–20.

Boyer, K. (2011). 'The way to break the taboo is to do the taboo thing' breastfeeding in public and citizen-activism in the UK. *Health and Place* 17(2): 430–437.

Boyer, K. (2012). Affect, corporeality and the limits of belonging: Breastfeeding in public in the contemporary UK. *Health and Place* 18(3): 552–560.

Boyer, K. (2014). 'Neoliberal motherhood': Workplace lactation and changing conceptions of working motherhood in the contemporary US. *Feminist Theory* 15(3): 269–288.

Boyer, K. and Spinney, J. (2016). Motherhood, mobility and materiality: Material entanglements, journey-making and the process of 'becoming mother'. *Environment and Planning D: Society and Space* 34(6):1113–1131.

Braidotti, R. (1994). *Nomadic subjects: Embodiment and sexual difference in contemporary feminist theory*. New York, NY: Columbia University Press.

Braidotti, R. (2002). *Metamorphoses: Towards a materialist theory of becoming*. Cambridge, UK: Polity Press.

Braidotti, R. (2003). Becoming woman: Or sexual difference revisited. *Theory, Culture & Society* 20(3): 43–64.

Braun, B. (2004). Modalities of posthumanism. *Environment and Planning A* 36(8): 1352–1355.

Braun, B. (2015). THE 2013 ANTIPODE RGS-IBG LECTURE New Materialisms and neoliberal natures. *Antipode* 47(1): 1–14.

Bray, A. and Colebrook, C. (1998). The haunted flesh: Corporeal feminism and the politics of (dis) embodiment. *Signs: Journal of Women in Culture and Society* 24(1): 35–67.

Breastfeeding Matters. (2009). The quintessence breastfeeding challenge history. Available at http://www.breastfeedingmatters.ca/html/challenge-history.html (accessed 9 June 2009).

Brown, A. (2016). *Breastfeeding uncovered: Who really decides how we feed our babies?* London, UK: Pinter and Martin.

Brown, A. (forthcoming). Breastfeeding and modern parenting culture: When worlds collide. In Dowling, S., Pontin, D. and Boyer, K. (eds.), *Social experiences of breastfeeding: Building bridges between research, policy and practice.* Bristol, UK: Policy Press.

Brown, M. (2004). Between neoliberalism and cultural conservatism: Spatial divisions and multiplications of hospice labor in the United States. *Gender, Place and Culture* 11(1): 67–81.

Buchanan, I. and Colebrook, C. (2000) *Deleuze and feminist theory.* Edinburgh, UK: Edinburgh University Press.

Buck-Morss, S. (1989). *The dialectics of seeing: Walter Benjamin and the Arcades Project.* Cambridge, MA: MIT Press.

Bureau of Labor Statistics. (2006). Labor force participation rates of mothers. *The Editors Desk (TED)*, available at http://www.bls.gov/opub/ted/2006/dec/wk1/art01.htm (accessed 20 August 2012).

Burgess, R. (1988). Conversations with a purpose: The ethnographic interview in educational research. *Studies in qualitative methodology* 1(1): 137–155.

Buser, M. (2014) Thinking through non-representational and affective atmospheres in planning theory and practice. *Planning Theory* 13(3): 227–243.

Buser, M., Bonura, C., Fannin, M. and Boyer, K. (2013). Cultural activism and the politics of place-making. *City* 17(5): 606–627.

Butler, J. (1993). *Bodies that matter: On the discursive limits of sex.* London, UK: Routledge.

Cardiff Council Breastfeeding Strategy. (2007). Executive Business Meeting, report of corporate director, *Cardiff City Council,* 22 November 2007, City Hall, Cardiff.

Carpenter, F. (2006). (L)Activists and lattes: Breastfeeding advocacy as domestic performance. *Women and Performance* 16(3): 347–367.

Carsten, J. (2004). *After kinship Cambridge.* Cambridge, UK: Cambridge University Press.

Carter, P. (1995). *Feminism, breasts and breast-feeding.* New York, NY: St. Martin's.

Cassidy, T. and El Tom, A., eds. (2015). *Ethnographies of breastfeeding: Cultural contexts and confrontations.* New York, NY: Bloomsbury Publishing.

Castree, N. and Nash, C. (2006). Posthuman geographies. *Social and Cultural Geography* 7(4): 501–504.

Centers for Disease Control. (2012). Breastfeeding report, available at http://www.cdc.gov/breastfeeding/data/reportcard.htm (accessed 19 August 2012).

Chakraborty, K. (2009). 'The good Muslim girl': Conducting qualitative participatory research to understand the lives of young Muslim women in the busses of Kolkata. *Children's Geographies* 7(4): 421–434.

Chouinard, V. (2004). Making feminist sense of the state and citizenship. In Staheli, L., Kofman, E. and Peake, L. (eds.), *Mapping women, making politics: Feminist perspectives on political geography.* New York, NY: Routledge, pp. 227–243.

Chung, M., Raman, G., Chew, P., Magula, N., Trikalinos, T., & Lau, J. (2007). Breastfeeding and maternal and infant health outcomes in developed countries. American Academy of Pediatrics *Grand Rounds*, 18(2): 15–16.

Cixous, H. (1976). The Laugh of the Medusa. *Signs* 1(4): 875–893.

Clarke, A. (2004). Maternity and materiality: Becoming a mother in consumer culture. In Taylor, J., Layne, L. and Wozniak, D. (eds.), *Consuming motherhood.* New Brunswick, NJ: Rutgers University Press, pp. 55–71.

Cockburn, C. and Ormrod, S. (1993). *Gender and technology in the making.* Thousand Oaks, CA: Sage.

Codd, J. (2008). Picnic protest at breastfeeding ban. *Dorset Echo,* 12 July, available at thisisdorset.net (accessed 8 June 2009).

Cohany, S. R., and Sok, E. (2007). Trends in labor force participation of married mothers of infants. *Monthly Labor Review* 130: 9.

Colebrook, C. (2008). On not becoming man: The materialist politics of unactualized potential. In Alaimo, S. and Hekman, S. J. (eds.), *Material feminisms.* Bloomington, IN: Indiana University Press, pp. 52–84.

Collins, P. H. (1994). Shifting the center: Race, class, and feminist theorizing about motherhood. In Glenn, E. N., Chang, G. and Forcey, L. R. (eds.), *Mothering: Ideology, experience, and agency.* London, UK: Routledge, pp. 45–65.

Colls, R. (2006). Outsize/outside: Bodily bignesses and the emotional experiences of British women shopping for clothes. *Gender, Place & Culture* 13(5): 529–545.

Colls, R. (2007). Materialising bodily matter: Intra-action and the embodiment of 'fat'. *Geoforum* 38(2): 353–365.

Colls, R. (2012). Feminism, bodily difference and non-representational geographies. *Transactions of the Institute of British Geographers* 37(3): 430–445.

Colls, R. and Fannin, M. (2013). Placental surfaces and the geographies of bodily interiors. *Environment and Planning A* 45(5): 1087–1104.

Conradson, D. (2003). Spaces of care in the city: The place of a community drop-in centre. *Social and Cultural Geography* 4(4): 507–525.

Cook, E. (2016). Poetry, breastfeeding and sex. *The Guardian* [online] 13 February, available at https://www.theguardian.com/lifeandstyle/2016/feb/13/poetry-breast-feeding-and-sex (accessed 16 October 2017).

Coole, D. and Frost, S., eds. (2010). *New materialisms: Ontology, agency, and politics.* Durham, NC and London, UK: Duke University Press.

Copeman, J. (2009). Introduction: Blood donation, bioeconomy, culture. *Body and Society* 15(2): 1–28.

Cowan, R. S. (1983). *More work for mother: The ironies of household technology from the open hearth to the microwave.* New York, NY: Basic Books.

Cresswell, T. (1996). *Place/out of place: Geography, ideology and transgression.* Minneapolis, MN: University of Minnesota Press.

Cresswell, T. (2006). *On the move: Mobility in the modern western world.* London, UK: Routledge.

Cresswell, T. (2010). Towards a politics of mobility. *Environment and Planning D: Society and Space* 28(1): 17–31.

Crompton, R. (2006). *Employment and the family.* Cambridge UK: Cambridge University Press.

Davidson, J. (2001). Pregnant pauses: Agoraphobic embodiment and the limits of (im) pregnability. *Gender, Place and Culture: A Journal of Feminist Geography* 8(3): 283–297.

Davidson, J. and Milligan, C. (2004). Embodying emotion sensing space: Introducing emotional geographies. *Social and Cultural Geography* 5(4): 523–532.

Davies, K. (1990). *Women, time, and the weaving of the strands of everyday life.* Farnham, UK: Gower Publishing Company.

Davis, T. (1995). The diversity of queer politics and the redefinition of sexual identity and community in urban spaces. In Bell, D. and Valentine G. (eds.), *Mapping desire: Geographies of sexuality*. London, UK: Routledge, pp. 284–303.

Deacon, A. (2000). Learning from the US? The influence of American ideas upon 'new labour' thinking on welfare reform. *Policy & Politics* 28(1): 5–18.

Deleuze, G. (1990). *Pourparlers*. Paris, France: Les Éditions de Minuit.

Deleuze, G. (1991). *Empiricism and subjectivity: An essay on Hume's theory of human nature*. Translated by Constantin V. Boundas. New York, NY: Columbia University Press.

Deleuze, G. (1994). *Difference and repetition*. Translated by Paul Patton. New York, NY: Columbia University Press.

Deleuze, G. and Guattari, F. (1983). *Anti-Oedipus: Capitalism and schizophrenia*. Translated by Robert Hurley, Mark Seem and Helen R. Lane. Minneapolis, MN: University of Minnesota Press.

Deleuze, G. and Guattari, F. (2004). *A thousand plateaus, capitalism and schizophrenia*. London, UK: Continuum.

DeNavas-Walt, C., Proctor, B. and Smith, J. (2011). *Income, poverty and health insurance coverage in the United States: 2010*. Washington, DC: US Department of Commerce, Economics and Statistics Administration, US Census Bureau.

Department of Health. (2003). Infant feeding recommendations. Available at http://webarchive.nationalarchives.gov.uk/20120503221049/http://www.dh.gov.uk/en/Publicationsandstatistics/Publications/PublicationsPolicyAndGuidance/DH_4097197 (accessed 23 February 2018).

Dermott, E. (2008). *Intimate fatherhood: A sociological analysis*. New York, NY: Routledge.

Dewsbury, J-D. (2000). Performativity and the event: Enacting a philosophy. *Environment and Planning D: Society and Space* 18(4): 473–496.

Dolowitz, D., Greenwold, S. and Marsh, D. (1999), Policy transfer: Something old, something new, something borrowed, but why red, white and blue? *Parliamentary Affairs* 52(4): 719–730.

Domosh, M. and Seager, J. (2001). *Putting women in place: Feminist geographers make sense of the world*. New York, NY: Guilford.

Doucet, A. (2006). *Do men mother? Fathering, care and domestic responsibility*. Toronto, Canada: University of Toronto Press.

Douglas, M. (1966). *Purity and danger: An analysis of concepts of pollution and taboo*. London, UK: Routledge and Kegan Paul.

Dowling, R. (2000). Cultures of mothering and car use in suburban Sydney: A preliminary investigation. *Geoforum* 31(3): 345–353.

Dowling, S. (forthcoming). Moving beyond the 'yuk' factor: Ethical issues in breastmilk sharing and donation. In Wintrup, J. (ed.), *Ethics from the ground up*. London, UK: Palgrave.

Dowling, S. and Brown, A. (2013). An exploration of the experiences of mothers who breastfeed long-term: What are the issues and why does it matter? *Breastfeeding Medicine* 8(1): 45–52.

Dowling, S., Naidoo, J. and Pontin, D. (2012). Breastfeeding in public: Women's bodies, women's milk. In Smith P. H., Hausman, B. and Labbok, P. (eds.), *Beyond health, beyond choice: Breastfeeding constraints and realities,* 1st ed. New Brunswick, NJ: Rutgers University Press, pp. 249–258. Available at http://eprints.uwe.ac.uk/20867.

Driscoll, C. (2000). The woman in process: Deleuze, Kristeva and feminism. In Buchanan, I. and Colebrook, C. (eds.), *Deleuze and feminist theory.* Edinburgh, UK: Edinburgh University Press, pp. 64–83.

Duff, C. (2010). On the role of affect and practice in the production of place. *Environment and planning D: Society and Space* 28(5): 881.

Dyck, I. (1990). Space, time, and renegotiating motherhood: An exploration of the domestic workplace. *Environment and Planning D: Society and Space* 8(4): 459–483.

Dykes, F. (2003). Infant feeding initiative: A report evaluating the breastfeeding practice projects 1999–2002: Executive summary. Department of Health, UK.

Dykes, F. (2005). 'Supply' and 'demand': Breastfeeding as labour. *Social Science & Medicine* 60(10): 2283–2293.

Dykes, F. (2006). *Breastfeeding in hospital: Mothers, midwives and the production line.* London, UK: Routledge.

Edensor, T. (2006). Reconsidering national temporalities: Institutional times, everyday routines, serial spaces and synchronicities. *European Journal of Social Theory* 9(4): 525–545.

Edgar, A. and Sebring, F. (2005). Anatomy of a working breast. *New Beginnings* 22(2): 44–50.

Eldridge, A. (2010). Public panics: Problematic bodies in social space. *Emotion, Space and Society* 3(1): 40–44.

El-Khuffash, A. and Unger, S. (2012). The concept of milk kinship in Islam: Issues raised when offering preterm infants of Muslim families donor human milk. *Journal of Human Lactation* 28(2): 125–127.

England, K., ed. (1996). *Who will mind the baby? Geographies of child care and working mothers.* London, UK: Psychology Press.

'Ethnicity and National Identity in England and Wales, 2011', National Archives, Office of National Statistics, 2012.

Evans, K. (2010). Equality bill won't protect breastfeeding. *The Guardian*, 8 March, 17.

Ezz El Din, Z. M., Abd El Ghaffar, S. and El Gabry, E. K. (2004). Is stored expressed breast milk an alternative for working Egyptian mothers? *Journal of East Mediterranean Health* 10(6): 815–821.

Fannin, M. (2013). 'Investing in YOU!': The hoarding economy of commercial stem cell storage. *Body & Society* 19(4): 32–60.

Feinstein, J., Berkelhamer, J., Gruszka, M. E., Wong, C. and Cary, A. (1986). Factors related to early termination of breast-feeding in an urban population. *Pediatrics* 78(2): 210–215.

Fenster, T. (1999). *Gender, planning and human rights.* London, UK: Routledge.

Figes, K. (1998). *Life after birth: What even your friends won't tell you about motherhood.* London, UK: Penguin.

Fincher, R. and Jacobs, J. M., eds. (1998). *Cities of difference*. New York, NY: Guilford Press.

Fluri, J. (2006). 'Our website was revolutionary': Virtual spaces of representation and resistance. *ACME: An International E-Journal of Critical Geographies* 5(1): 89–111.

Foley, C., Caryn, H. and Wearing, S. (2007). Moving beyond conspicuous leisure consumption: Adolescent women, mobile phones and public space. *Leisure Studies* 26(2): 179–192.

Fox, B. (2006). Motherhood as a class act: The many ways in which 'intensive mothering' is entangled with social class. In Bezanson, K. and Luxton, M. (eds.), *Social reproduction: Feminist political economy challenges neo-liberalism*. Montreal and Kingston, Canada: McGill-Queen's Press, pp. 231–262.

Francis, J., Rogers, K., Dickton, D., Twedt, R. and Pardini, R. (2012). 'Decreasing retinol and a-tocopherol concentrations in human milk and infant formula using varied bottle systems'. *Maternal & Child Nutrition* 8(2): 215–224.

Fraser, M. (forthcoming). Lactation breaks: Employer's perspectives. In Dowling, S., Pontin, D. and Boyer, K. (eds.), *Social experiences of breastfeeding: Building bridges between research, policy and practice*. Bristol, UK: Policy Press.

Fraser, N. (1997). *Justice interruptus: Critical reflections on the 'postsocialist' condition*. New York, NY: Routledge.

Fuller, D. (2008). Public geographies: Taking stock. *Progress in Human Geography* 32(6): 834–844.

Gabb, J. (2005). Locating lesbian parent families: Everyday negotiations of lesbian motherhood in Britain. *Gender, Place & Culture* 12(4): 419–432.

Gallagher, M. (2008). Breastfeeding picnic 2008. Available at http://one-of-those-women.blogspot.com (accessed 5 June 2009).

Galtry, J. (2000). Extending the 'bright line': Feminism, breastfeeding and the workplace. *Gender & Society* 14(2): 295–317.

Gartner, L. M., Morton, J., Lawrence, R. A., Naylor, A. J., O'Hare, D., Schanler, R. J. and Eidelman, A. I. (2005). Breastfeeding and the use of human milk. *Pediatrics* 115(2): 496–506.

Gatrell, C. (2007). Secrets and lies: Breastfeeding and professional paid work. *Social Science and Medicine* 65(2): 393–404.

Geraghty, S., Khoury, J. and Kalkwarf, H. (2005). Human milk pumping rates of mothers of singletons and mothers of multiples. *Journal of Human Lactation* 21(4): 413–420.

Gibson-Graham, J. K. (2006). *A postcapitalist politics*. Minneapolis, MN: University of Minnesota Press.

Gilbert, M. (2001). From the 'walk for adequate welfare' to the 'march for our lives': Welfare rights organizing in the 1960s and 1990s. *Urban Geography* 22(5): 440–456.

Giles, F. (forthcoming). Making breastfeeding social, the role of brelfies in breastfeeding's burgeoning publics. In Dowling, S., Pontin, D. and Boyer, K. (eds.), *Social experiences of breastfeeding: Building bridges between research, policy and practice*. Bristol, UK: Policy Press.

Gill-Peterson, J. (2013). Haunting the queer spaces of AIDS remembering ACT UP/New York and an ethics for an endemic. *GLQ: A Journal of Lesbian and Gay Studies* 19(3): 279–300.

Goldman, A. S. (2000). Modulation of the gastrointestinal tract of infants by human milk, interfaces and interactions: An evolutionary perspective. *Journal of Nutrition* 130(2): 426–431.

Gorenstein, S. (2010). What we now know about feminist technologies. In Layne, L., Vostral, S. and Boyer, K. (eds.), *Feminist technology*. Champaign-Urbana, IL: University of Illinois Press, pp. 203–214.

Grant, A. (2016). 'I . . . don't want to see you flashing your bits around': Exhibitionism, othering and good motherhood in perceptions of public breastfeeding. *Geoforum* 71: 52–61.

Greed, C. (1994). *Women and planning: Creating gendered differences*. London, UK: Routledge.

Gregson, N. and Rose, G. (2000). Taking Butler elsewhere: Performativities, spatialities and subjectivities. *Environment and Planning D: Society and Space* 18(4): 433–452.

Groskop, V. (2010). Breastfeeding under wraps. *The Guardian* [online] 27 August, available at https://www.theguardian.com/lifeandstyle/2010/aug/27/breastfeeding-hooter-hiders (accessed 5 June 2011).

Grosz, E. (1994). *Volatile bodies: Towards a corporeal feminism*. Bloomington, IN: Indiana University Press.

Grosz, E. (1998). Bodies-Cities. In Pile, S. and Nast, H. (eds.), *Places through the body*. London, UK: Routledge, pp. 42–51.

Grosz, E. (2005). *Time travels: Feminism, nature, power*. Durham, NC: Duke University Press.

Guattari, F. (1995). *Chaosmosis: An ethico-aesthetic paradigm*. Bloomington, IN: Indiana University Press.

Hall, E. (2000). 'Blood, brain, and bones': Taking the body seriously in the geography of health and impairment. *Area* 32(1): 21–29.

Hansard of UK Parliament, House of Commons, July 16 (2007). Commons debates: Maternity leave, 16 July, available at http://www.publications.parliament.uk/pa/cm200607/cmhansrd/cm070716/text/70716w0011.htm (accessed 20 August 2012).

Harmon, A. (2005). 'Lactivists' taking their cause, and their babies, to the streets. *New York Times*, 7 June, available at http://www.nytimes.com/2005/06/07/nyregion/07nurse.html (accessed 27 July 2009).

Hausman, B. L. (2003). *Mother's milk: Breastfeeding controversies in American culture*. London, UK: Psychology Press, Routledge.

Hausman, B. L. (2004). The feminist politics of breastfeeding. *Australian Feminist Studies* (19): 273–285.

Hays, S. (1998). *The cultural contradictions of motherhood*. London, UK: Yale University Press.

Hays, S. (2004). *Flat broke with children*. Oxford, UK: Oxford University Press.

Health Inequalities. (2009). House of Commons Health Committee, 25 March. Available at http://www.publications.parliament.uk/pa/cm200809/cmselect/cmhealth/286/286.pdf (accessed 26 July 2010).

Helderman, R. (2004). Maryland moms say no to coverup at Starbucks women push chain for policy allowing public breast-feeding in all U.S. stores. *Washington Post*, 22 February, available at http://alloveralbany.com/archive/2008/02/22/got-milk-nurse-in-at-the-nys-museum (accessed 9 June 2009).

Hickey-Moody, A. (2013). Deleuze's children. *Educational Philosophy and Theory* 45(3): 272–286.

Holdsworth, C. (2013). *Family and intimate mobilities*. Basingstoke UK: Palgrave Macmillan.

Holloway, S. (1998). Local childcare cultures: Moral geographies of mothering and the social organisation of pre-school education. *Gender, Place and Culture: A Journal of Feminist Geography* 5(1): 29–53.

Holloway, S. (1999). Mother and worker? The negotiation of motherhood and paid employment in two urban neighbourhoods. *Urban Geography* 20(5): 438–460.

Hollway, W. and Featherstone, B. (1997). *Mothering and ambivalence*. London, UK: Psychology Press.

Holt, L. (2013). Exploring the emergence of the subject in power: Infant geographies. *Environment and Planning D: Society and Space* 31(4): 645–663.

Horta, B. L., Bahl, R., Martines, J. C. and Victora, C. G. (2007). *Evidence on the long-term effects of breastfeeding: Systematic reviews and meta-analyses*. Geneva, Switzerland: World Health Organisation.

Horwood, L. J, Darlow, B. A. and Mogridge, N. (2001). Breast milk feeding and cognitive ability at 7–8 years. *ADC Fetal & Neonatal Edition* 84(1): 23–27.

Hubbard, P. and Lilley, K. (2004). Pacemaking the modern city: The urban politics of speed and slowness. *Environment and Planning D: Society and Space* 22(2): 273–294.

Hyde, M. (2012). Regulating human products: Breastmilk as a product. In *Baby GAGA SAGA Workshop*. Keele, UK, Monday 26 March. Keele University's Gender Sexuality and Law research group.

Imrie, R. and Kumar, M. (1998). Focusing on disability and access in the built environment. *Disability & Society* 13(3): 357–374.

Irigaray, L. (1985). *Speculum of the other woman*. Ithaca, NY: Cornell University Press.

Irigaray, L. (2004). *Way of love*. London, UK: A&C Black.

Ishak, W. (2011). Oxytocin role in enhancing well-being: A literature review. *Journal of Affective Disorders* 130(1–2): 1–9.

Johnson, S., Leeming, D., Williamson, I. and Lyttle, S. (2012). Maintaining the 'good maternal body': Expressing milk as a way of negotiating the demands and dilemmas of early infant feeding. *Journal of Advanced Nursing* 69(3): 590–599.

Johnson, S., Williamson, I., Lyttle, S. and Leeming, D. (2009). Expressing yourself: A feminist analysis of talk around expressing breast milk. *Social Science and Medicine* 69(6):900–907.

Juhausz, S. (2003). Mother-writing and the narrative of maternal subjectivity. *Studies in Gender and Sexuality* 4(4): 395–425.

Jupp, E. (2017). Families, policies and place in times of austerity. *Area* 49(3): 266–272.

Kaplan, T. (1997). *Crazy for democracy: Women in grassroots movements*. New York, NY: Routledge.

Katz, C. and Monk, J., eds. (1993). *Full circles: Geographies of women over the life course*. London, UK: Routledge.

Keith, M. and Pile, S., eds. (2004). *Place and the politics of identity*. London, UK: Routledge.

Kelleher, C. M. (2006). The physical challenges of early breastfeeding. *Social Science & Medicine* 63(10): 2727–2738.

Kirsch, S. (2013). Cultural geography I. Materialist turns. *Progress in Human Geography* 37(3): 433–441.

Kitchin, R. and Tate, N. J. (2000). *Conducting research into human geography.* Upper Saddle River, NJ: Prentice Hall Harlow.

Kobayashi, A. and Peake, L. (2000). Racism out of place: Thoughts on whiteness and an antiracist geography in the new millennium. *Annals of the Association of American Geographers* 90(2): 392–403.

La Leche League International. (2003). Breastfeeding statistics. *LLLI Center for Breastfeeding Information.* Available at http://www.llli.org/cbi/bfstats03.html (accessed 9 August 2010).

Landivar, L. (2011). The impact of the 2007–2009 recession on Mothers' Employment, Industry and Occupation Statistics Branch, Social, Economic, and Housing Statistics Division U.S. Census Bureau, Working Paper 2011–29. Available at www.census.gov/hhes/www/ . . . /NCFR%20Landivar%20111011.docx (accessed 20 August 2012).

Lane, A., Luminet, O., Rimé, B., Gross, J. J., de Timary, P. and Mikolajczak, M. (2013). Oxytocin increases willingness to socially share one's emotions. *International Journal of Psychology* 48(4): 676–681.

Lapore, J. (2009). Baby food: If breast is best, why are women bottling their milk? *New Yorker,* 19 January, available at http://www.newyorker.com/reporting/2009/01/19/090119fa_fact_lepore (accessed 12 September 2012).

Latham, A. (2003). Research, performance, and doing human geography: Some reflections on the diary-autograph, diary-interview method. *Environment and Planning A* 35(11): 1993–2017.

Latham, A. and McCormack, D. (2004). Moving cities: Rethinking the materialities of urban geographies. *Progress in Human Geography* 28(6): 701–724.

Layne, L., Vostral, S. and Boyer, K., eds. (2010). *Feminist technology.* Champaign-Urbana: University of Illinois Press.

Leeming, D., Williamson, I., Lyttle, S. and Johnson, S. (2013). Socially sensitive lactation: Exploring the social context of breastfeeding. *Psychology & Health* 28(4): 450–468.

Lenz-Taguchi, H. (2012). A diffractive and Deleuzian approach to analysing interview data. *Feminist Theory* 13(3): 265–281.

Li, R., Darling, N., Maurice, E., Barker, L. and Grummer-Strawn, L. M. (2005). Breastfeeding rates in the United States by characteristics of the child, mother, or family: The 2002 National Immunization Survey. *Pediatrics* 115(1): 31–37.

Li, R., Fein, S. B., Chen, J. and Grummer-Strawn, L. M. (2008). Why mothers stop breastfeeding: Mothers' self-reported reasons for stopping during the first year. *Pediatrics* 122(2): 69–76.

Lister, R. (2008). Gender, citizenship and social justice in the Nordic welfare states: A view from the outside. In Melby, K., Ravn, A-B. and Wetterberg, C. (eds.), *Gender equality and welfare politics in Scandinavia: The limits of political ambition?* Bristol, UK: Polity, pp. 215–222.

Loewen Walker, R. (2014). The living present as a materialist feminist temporality. *Women: A Cultural Review* 25(1): 46–61.

Longhurst, R. (2000). Corporeographies' of pregnancy: 'Bikini babes'. *Environment and Planning D: Society and Space* 18(4): 453–472.

Longhurst, R. (2001). *Bodies: Exploring fluid boundaries.* New York, NY and London, UK: Routledge.

Longhurst, R. (2008). *Maternities: Gender, bodies, and spaces.* New York, NY and London, UK: Routledge.

Longhurst, R. (2013). Using Skype to mother: Bodies, emotions, visuality, and screens. *Environment and Planning D: Society and Space* 31(4): 664–679.

Lorimer, H. (2008). Cultural geography: Non-representational conditions and concerns. *Progress in Human Geography* 32(4): 551–559.

Lucas, A., Morley, R., Cole, T. J. and Gore, S. M. (1994). A randomised multicentre study of human milk versus formula and later development in preterm infants. *ADC Fetal & Neonatal edition* 70(2): 141–146.

Lupton, D. (2013). Infant embodiment and interembodiment: A review of sociocultural perspectives. *Childhood* 20(1): 37–50.

Luzia, K. (2010). Travelling in your backyard: The unfamiliar places of parenting. *Social & Cultural Geography* 11(4): 359–375.

Luzia, K. (2013). 'Beautiful but tough terrain': The uneasy geographies of same-sex parenting. *Children's Geographies* 11(2): 243–255.

Madge, C. and O'Connor, H. (2005). Mothers in the making? Exploring liminality in cyber/space. *Transactions of the Institute of British Geographers* 30(1): 83–97.

Mahon-Daly, P. and Andrews, G. J. (2002). Liminality and breastfeeding: Women negotiating space and two bodies. *Health & Place* 8(2): 61–76.

Malik, A. N. J. and Cutting, W. A. M. (1988). Breast feeding: The baby friendly initiative. *British Medical Journal* 316(7144): 1548–1549.

Mangold, S. (2009). Get your nipples out of my Facebook. *The Guardian* [online] 7 January, available at https://www.theguardian.com/commentisfree/cifamerica/2009/jan/07/facebook-breastfeeding-photographs (accessed 8 June 2009).

Marshall, J. L., Godfrey, M. and Renfrew, M. J. (2007). Being a 'good mother': Managing breastfeeding and merging identities. *Social Science & Medicine* 65(10): 2147–2159.

Massey, D. (1984). *Spatial divisions of labor.* New York, NY: Methuen.

Massey, D. (1993). Power-geometry and a progressive sense of place. In Bird, J., Curtis, B., Putnam, T., Robertson, G. and Tickner, L. (eds.), *Mapping the futures: Local cultures, global change.* London, UK: Routledge, pp. 59–69.

Massey, D. (2006). Landscape as a provocation reflections on moving mountains. *Journal of Material Culture*, 11(1–2): 33–48.

Mathers, J., Parry, J. and Jones, S. (2008). Exploring resident (non-)participation in the UK New Deal for Communities Regeneration Programme. *Urban Studies* 45(3): 591–606.

May, T. (2003). When is a Deleuzian becoming? *Continental Philosophy Review*, 36(2): 139–153.

McAndrew, F., Thompson, J., Fellows, L., Large, A., Speed, M. and Renfrew, M. (2012). *Infant feeding survey 2010.* Leeds, UK: Health and Social Care Information Centre.

McCarter-Spaulding, D. (2008). Is breastfeeding fair? Tensions in feminist perspectives on breastfeeding and the family. *Journal of Human Lactation* 24(2): 206–212.

McDowell, L. (2009). *Working bodies: Interactive service employment and workplace identities*. Chichester, UK and Malden, MA: Wiley-Blackwell.

McDowell, L., Ray, K., Perrons, D., Fagan, C. and Ward, K. (2005). Women's paid work and moral economies of care. *Social & Cultural Geography* 6(2): 219–235.

McDowell, L., Ward, K., Perrons, D., Ray, K. and Fagan, C. (2006). Place, class and local circuits of reproduction: Exploring the social geography of middle-class childcare in London. *Urban Studies* 43(12): 2163–2182.

McDowell, M., Wang, C-Y. and Kennedy-Stephenson, J. (2008). Breastfeeding in the United States: Findings from the National Health and Nutrition Examination Surveys, 1999–2006. *NCHS Data Brief #5 National Center for Health Statistics of the Centers for Disease Control and Prevention*, available at http://www.cdc.gov/nchs/data/databriefs/db05.htm (accessed 21 August 2012).

McIntyre, E., Hiller, J. and Turnbull, D. (1999). Determinants of infant feeding practices in a low socio-economic area: Identifying environmental barriers to breast-feeding. *ANZJ Public Health* 23(2): 207–209.

McNish, H. (2013). Embarrassed || Spoken Word by @holliepoetry, YouTube, available at https://www.youtube.com/watch?v=KiS8q_fifa0 (accessed 16 October 2017).

Megginson, S. (2016). 'Embarrassed'. The Facebook video everyone is talking about. *MamaMia:What women are talking about,* available at http://www.mamamia.com.au/hollie-mcnish-embarrassed/ (accessed 16 October 2017).

Mennella, J. A. and Beauchamp, G. K. (1991). Maternal diet alters the sensory qualities of human milk and the nursling's behavior. *Pediatrics* 88(4): 737–744.

Miller, D. (1998). *A theory of shopping*. Cambridge, UK: Polity Press.

Miller, T. (2005). *Making sense of motherhood: A narrative approach*. Cambridge, UK: Cambridge University Press.

Milligan, C. (2001). *Geographies of care: Space, place, and the voluntary sector*. Hants, UK and Burlington, VT: Ashgate.

Milligan, C. (2003). Location or dis-location? Towards a conceptualization of people and place in the care-giving experience. *Social & Cultural Geography* 4(4): 455–470.

Mink, G. (1998). The lady and the tramp (II): Feminist welfare politics, poor single mothers and the challenge of welfare justice. *Feminist Studies* 24(1): 55–64.

Mitchell, D. (2003). *The right to the city*. Guilford, London, UK: Guildford Press.

Mitchell, K., Marston, S. A. and Katz, C., eds. (2004). *Life's work: Geographies of social reproduction*. Oxford, UK: Blackwell.

Morse, J. and Bottorff, J. L. (1988). The emotional experience of breast expression. *Journal of Midwifery & Women's Health* 33(4): 165–170.

Moss, P. and Dyck, E. (2003). Embodying social geography. In Anderson, K., Domosh, M., Pile, S. and Thrift, N. (eds.), *Handbook of cultural geography*. London, UK: Sage. pp. 58–73.

Mouffe, C. (2005). *On the political*. London, UK: Routledge.

Murphy-Geiss, G. (2010). Muslim motherhood traditions in changing contexts. In O'Reilly, A. (ed.), *Twenty-first-century motherhood: Experience, identity, policy, agency*. New York, NY: Columbia University Press, pp. 40–56.

Nahman, M. R. (2013). *Extractions*. London, UK: Palgrave Macmillan UK.

Naples, N. (1998). *Community activism and feminist politics*. New York, NY: Routledge.

Nast, H. and Pile, S. (1998) *Places through the body*. London, UK: Routledge.

National Childbirth Trust. (2009). Mother and Baby survey reveals mothers worries about breastfeeding in public. Available at http://nctwatch.wordpress.com (accessed 7 May 2010).

National Conference of State Legislatures. (2009) Available at http://www.ncsl.org/research/health/breastfeeding-state-laws.aspx (accessed 23 February 2018).

Newell, L. (2013). Disentangling the politics of breastfeeding. *Children's Geographies* 11(2): 256–261.

Noddings, N. (2001). The care tradition: Beyond 'add women and stir'. *Theory into Practice* 40(1): 29–34.

O'Reilly, A. ed. (2010). *The 21st century motherhood movement*. Ontario, Canada: Demeter Press.

O'Sullivan, S. (2006). Pragmatics for the production of subjectivity: Time for probe-heads. *Journal for Cultural Research* 10(4): 309–322.

Pain, R. (2006). Paranoid parenting? Rematerializing risk and fear for children. *Social & Cultural Geography* 7(2): 221–243.

Pain, R., Bailey, C. and Mowl, G. (2001). Infant feeding in North East England: Contested spaces of reproduction. *Area* 33(3): 261–272.

Parker, R. and Bar, V. (1996). Torn in two: The experience of maternal ambivalence. *Journal of Analytical Psychology* 41(4): 611–612.

Payne, D. and Nichols, D. (2010). Managing breastfeeding and work: A Foucauldian secondary analysis. *Journal of Advanced Nursing* 66(8): 1810–1818.

Pearlman, S.F. (2010). Mother-talk: Conversations with mothers of female-to-male transgender children. In O'Reilly, A. (ed.), *Twenty-first-century motherhood: Experience, identity, policy, agency*. New York, NY: Columbia University Press, pp. 72–89.

Perrons, D. (2000). Care, paid work, and leisure: Rounding the triangle. *Feminist Economics* 6(1): 105–114.

Perrons, D., Fagan, C., McDowell, L., Ray, K. and Ward, K. (2006). *Gender divisions and working time in the new economy*. Cheltenham, UK: Edward Elgar Press.

Pilkington, E. (2006). Lactivists fight for the right to breastfeed. *The Guardian* Available at https://www.theguardian.com/world/2006/nov/24/usa.topstories3 (accessed 21 March 2018). 23 November, 7.

Popke, J. (2009). Geography and ethics: Non-representational encounters, collective responsibility and economic difference. *Progress in Human Geography* 1(33): 81–90.

Pratt, G. (2012). *Families apart: Migrant mothers and the conflicts of labor and love*. Minneapolis, MN: University of Minnesota Press.

Pratt, M. B. (1992). Identity: Skin, blood, heart. In Crowley, H. and Himmelweit, S. (eds.), *Knowing women: Feminism and knowledge*. Cambridge, UK: Polity Press, pp. 11–60.

Prentice, A., Prentice, A. M. and Whitehead, R. G. (1981). Breast-milk fat concentrations of rural African women. *British journal of Nutrition* 45(3): 495–503.

Raisler, J. (2000). Against the odds: Breastfeeding experiences of low income mothers. *Journal of Midwifery & Women's Health* 45(3): 253–263.

Rancière, J. (2010). *Dissensus: On politics and aesthetics*. London, UK: Continuum.

Raphael-Leff, J. (2009). Editorial: Maternal subjectivity. *Studies in the Maternal* 1(1): 1–15.

Rasmussen, K. and Geraghty, S. R. (2011). The quiet revolution: Breastfeeding transformed with the use of breast pumps. *American Journal of Public Health* 101(8): 1356–1359.

Ray, B. and Rose, D. (2000). Cities of the everyday: Socio-spatial perspectives on gender, difference and diversity. In Bunting, T. and Filion, P. (eds.), *Canadian cities in transition: The twenty-first century*. Toronto, Canada: Oxford University Press, pp. 402–424.

Reiger, K. (2000). Reconceiving citizenship. *Feminist Theory* 1(3): 309–327.

Reiger, K. (2006). The neoliberal quickstep: Contradictions in Australian maternity care policy. *Health Sociology Review, Special Issue, Childbirth, Politics and the Culture of Risk* 15(4): 330–340.

Reiger, K., Garvan, J. and Temel, S. (2009). Rethinking care: A critical analysis of family policies and the negotiation of dependency. *Just Policy* 50: 16–22.

Rich, A. (1995). *Of woman born: Motherhood as experience and institution*. London, UK: WW Norton & Company.

Roberts, M. (2007). Capitalism, psychiatry, and schizophrenia: A critical introduction to Deleuze and Guattari's Anti-Oedipus. *Nursing Philosophy* 8(2): 114–127.

Roberts, R. (2004). Do me a favor, keep your lid on your double latte. *Washington Post*, 10 August, available at http://www.washingtonpost.com/wp-dyn/articles/A55338-2004Aug10.html (accessed 23 February 2018).

Robinson, C. (2016). Misshapen motherhood: Placing breastfeeding distress. *Emotion Space and Society*. ePub ahead of print DOI: https://doi.org/10.1016/j.emospa.2016.09.008.

Robinson, K. (2001). Unsolicited narratives from the internet: A rich source of qualitative data. *Qualitative Health Research* 11(5): 706–714.

Robinson, V. S. (2006). Veronika Sophia Robinson, author and novelist. Available at http://veronikarobinson.blogspot.co.uk/ (accessed 5 June 2009).

Roe, E. J. and Greenhough, B. (2006). Towards a geography of bodily technologies. *Environment and Planning A* 38(3): 416–422.

Rollins, N. C., Bhandari, N., Hajeebhoy, N., Horton, S., Lutter, C. K., Martines, J. C., Piwoz, E. G., Richter, L. M., Victora, C. G. and The Lancet Breastfeeding Series Group. (2016). 'Why invest, and what it will take to improve breastfeeding practices?' *The Lancet* 387(10017): 491–504.

Ronander, K. (2010). The restorative dynamic of walking together. *The Qualitative Researcher* 12: 3–5.

Rose, G. (1993). *Feminism & geography: The limits of geographical knowledge*. Minneapolis, MN: University of Minnesota Press.

Rose, G. (2003). Family photographs and domestic spacings: A case study. *Transactions of the Institute of British Geographers* 28(1): 5–18.

Rose, G. (2004). 'Everyone's cuddled up and it just looks really nice': An emotional geography of some mums and their family photos. *Social & Cultural Geography* 5(4): 549–564.

Rose, G., Hardy, S. and Wiedmer, C. (2005). *Motherhood and space: Configurations of the maternal through politics, home and the body*. New York, NY: Palgrave Macmillan.

Rose, N. (1999). *Powers of freedom: Reframing political thought*. Cambridge, UK: Cambridge University Press.

Rosin, H. (2009). The case against breastfeeding. *The Atlantic*, April, available at http://www.theatlantic.com/magazine/archive/2009/04/the-case-against-breast-feeding/307311/ (accessed 12 September 2009).

Rothschild, J. (1999). *Design and feminism: Re-visioning spaces, places, and everyday things*. New Brunswick, NJ: Rutgers.

Royal New Zealand Plunket Society. (2010). Breastfeeding data: Analysis of 2004–2009 data. Available at https://www.plunket.org.nz/news-and-research/research-from-plunket/plunket-breastfeeding-data-analysis/ (accessed 01 March 2018).

Ruddick, S. (1980). Maternal thinking. *Feminist Studies* 6(2): 342–367.

Ruddick, S. (1989). *Maternal thinking: Towards a politics of peace*. Boston, MA: Beacon Press.

Ruddick, S. (1996). Constructing difference in public spaces: Race, class and gender as interlocking systems. *Urban Geography* 17(2): 132–151.

Saldanha, A. (2005). Trance and visibility at dawn: Racial dynamics in Goa's rave scene. *Social and Cultural Geography* 6(5): 707–721.

Scariati, P.D., Grummer-Strawn, L. and Beck Fein, S. (1997). A longitudinal analysis of infant morbidity and the extent of breastfeeding in the United States. *Pediatrics* 99(6): 5.

Schalch, K. (2006). Airport protests back right to breastfeed. NPR, 21 November, available at http://www.npr.org/templates/story/story.php?storyId=6522262 (accessed 27 July 2009).

Schmidt, S. (1998). 'Private' acts in 'public' spaces: Parks in turn-of-the-century Montreal. In Myers, T., Boyer, K., Poutanen, M. A. and Watt, S. (eds.), *Power, place and identity: Historical studies of social and legal regulation in Quebec*. Montreal, Canada: Montreal History Group, pp. 129–149.

Schmied, V. and Barclay, L. (1999). Connection and pleasure, disruption and distress: Women's experiences of breastfeeding. *Journal of Human Lactation* 15(4): 325–334.

Schmied, V. and Lupton, D. (2001). Blurring the boundaries: Breastfeeding and maternal subjectivity. *Sociology of Health and Illness* 23(2): 234–250.

Schwanen, T., Kwan, M. and Ren, F. (2008). How fixed is fixed? Gender rigidity of space-time constraints and geographies of everyday activities. *Geoforum* 39(6): 2109–2121.

Scott, J. and Mostyn, T. (2003). Women's experiences of breastfeeding in a bottle-feeding culture. *Journal of Human Lactation* 19(3): 270–277.

Serres, M. (1995). *Genesis*. Ann Arbor, MI: University of Michigan Press.

Sevenhuijsen, S. (2003). The place of care: The relevance of the feminist ethic of care for social policy. *Feminist Theory* 4(2): 179–197.

Shabo, V. (2011). The good, the bad and the hope for breastfeeding rights. *National Partnership for Women and Families* 22(8), available at http://www.nationalpart-nership.org (accessed 01 March 2018).

Shakespeare, T. and Watson, N. (2002). The social model of disability: An outdated ideology? *Research in Social Science and Disability* 2(28): 9–28.

Sharp, J. (2009). Geography and gender: What belongs to feminist geography? Emotion, power and change. *Progress in Human Geography* 33(1): 74–80.

Sheeshka, J., Potter, B., Norrie, E., Valaitis, R., Adams, G. and Kuczynski, L. (2001). Women's experiences breastfeeding in public places. *Journal of Human Lactation* 17(1): 31–38.

Shildrick, M. (2010). Becoming-maternal: Things to do with Deleuze. *Studies in the Maternal* 2(1): 1–8.

Simpson, P. (2013). Ecologies of experience: Materiality, sociality and the embodied experience of (street) performing. *Environment and Planning A* 45(1): 180–196.

Smith, J. (2004). Mother's milk and markets. *Australian Feminist Studies* 19(45): 369–379.

Smith, P. H., Hausman, B. and Labbok, M., eds. (2012). *Beyond health, beyond choice: Breastfeeding constraints and realities*. New Brunswick, NJ: Rutgers University Press.

Smyth, L. (2008). Gendered spaces and intimate citizenship: The case of breastfeeding. *European Journal of Women's Studies* 15(2): 83–99.

Smyth, L. (2012). *The demands of motherhood*. Hampshire: Palgrave.

Spain, D. (2001). *How women saved the city*. Minneapolis, MN: University of Minnesota Press.

Spencer, R. (2008). Research methodologies to investigate the experience of breastfeeding: A discussion paper. *Nursing Studies* 45(12): 1823–1830.

Spinney, J. (2006). A place of sense: A kinaesthetic ethnography of cyclists on Mont Ventoux. *Environment and Planning D: Society and Space* 24(5): 709–732.

Spinney, J. (2010). Performing resistance? Re-reading practices of urban cycling on London's South Bank. *Environment and Planning A* 42(12): 2914–2937.

Stanton, R. (2011). US Breastfeeding Committee's Public Comments on the Department of Labor's Request for Information. Available at http://www.usbreastfeeding. org/Employment/WorkplaceSupport/WorkplaceSupportinFederalLaw/tabid/175/ Default.aspx (accessed 20 August 2012).

Stark, H. (2017). *Feminist theory after Deleuze*. London, UK: Bloomsbury.

Statistics Canada Health. (2010). Health at a glance breastfeeding trends. Available at http://www.statcan.gc.ca/pub/82-624-x/82-624-x2013001-eng.htm (accessed 2 January 2015).

Stearns, C. (1999). Breastfeeding and the good maternal body. *Gender and Society* 13(3): 308–325.

Stewart, K. (2011). Atmospheric attunements. *Environment and Planning D: Society and Space* 29(3): 445–453.

Stewart-Knox, B., Gardiner, K. and Wright, M. (2003). What is the problem with breast-feeding? A qualitative analysis of infant feeding perceptions. *Journal of Nutrition and Dietetics* 16(4): 265–273.

Sweney, M. (2008). Mums furious as Facebook removes breastfeeding photos. *The Guardian* [online] 30 December, available at https://www.theguardian.com/ media/2008/dec/30/facebook-breastfeeding-ban (accessed 01 March 2018).

Taguchi, L. (2012). A diffractive and Deleuzian approach to analysing interview data. *Feminist Theory* 13(3): 265–281.

Talbot, D. (2013). Early parenting and the urban experience: Risk, community, play and embodiment in an East London neighbourhood. *Children's Geographies* 11(2): 230–242.

Tarrant, R. and Kearney, J. (2008). Public health nutrition: Breastfeeding practices in Ireland. *Proceedings of the Nutrition Society* 67(4): 371–380.

Taylor, J. S., Layne, L. L. and Wozniak, D. F., eds. (2004). *Consuming motherhood*. New Brunswick, NJ: Rutgers University Press.

Taylor, Y. (2009). *Lesbian and gay parenting: Securing social and educational capital*. London, UK: Palgrave Macmillan.

Thien, D. (2005). After or beyond feeling? A consideration of affect and emotion in geography. *Area* 37(4): 450–456.

Thomson, R., Kehily, M. J., Hadfield, L. and Sharpe, S. (2011). *Making modern mothers*. Bristol, UK: The Policy Press.

Thrift, N. (2004). Driving in the city. *Theory, Culture & Society* 21(4–5): 41–59.

Tolia-Kelly, D. P. (2006). Affect – an ethnocentric encounter? Exploring the 'universalist' imperative of emotional/affectual geographies. *Area* 38(2): 213–217.

Tolia-Kelly, D. P. (2010). The geographies of cultural geography I: Identities, bodies and race. *Progress in Human Geography* 34(3): 358–367.

Tolia-Kelly, D. P. (2013). The geographies of cultural geography III: Material geographies, vibrant matters and risking surface geographies. *Progress in Human Geography* 37(1): 153–160.

Tomlinson, J. (2007). Employment regulation, welfare and gender regimes: A comparative analysis of women's working-time patterns and work-life balance in the UK and the US. *International Journal of Human Resource Management* 18(3): 401–415.

Tomori, C. (2014). *Nighttime breastfeeding: An American cultural dilemma*. Oxford, UK and New York, NY: Berghahn Books.

Tomori, C. (forthcoming). Changing culture of nighttime breastfeeding and sleep in the US. In Dowling, S., Pontin, D. and Boyer, K. (eds.), *Social experiences of breastfeeding: Building bridges between research, policy and practice*. Bristol, UK: Policy Press.

Torjesen, I. (2016). Austerity cuts are eroding benefits of Sure Start children's centres. *BMJ: British Medical Journal* [online] 352, DOI: 10.1136/bmj.i335.

Trade Union Congress (TUC). (2013). Men in their early 40s have longest commutes. Available at www.tuc.org.uk/workplace-issues/work-life-balance/men-their-early-40s-have-longest-commutes (accessed 20 August 2015).

Tran, M. (2014). Claridge's hotel criticised after telling breastfeeding woman to cover up. *The Guardian* [online] 2 December, available at https://www.theguardian.com/lifeandstyle/2014/dec/02/claridges-hotel-breastfeeding-woman-cover-up (accessed 24 January 2016).

UNICEF. (2010). The Baby Friendly Initiative. Available at https://www.unicef.org.uk/babyfriendly/ (accessed 2 January 2015).

Urry, J. (2000). *Sociology beyond societies: Mobilities for the twenty-first century*. London, UK: Routledge.

US Centers for Disease Control and Prevention. (2012). Breastfeeding report cards. Available at https://www.cdc.gov/breastfeeding/data/reportcard.htm (accessed 2 January 2015).

Valentine, G. (1997). 'My son's a bit dizzy'. 'My wife's a bit soft': Gender, children and cultures of parenting. *Gender, Place and Culture* 4(1): 37–62.

Valentine, G. (2004). *Public space and the culture of childhood*. London, UK: Ashgate.

Van der Tuin, I. and Dolphijn, R. (2012). *New materialism: Interviews & cartographies*. London, UK: Open Humanities Press.

Van Esterik, P (1996) Expressing ourselves: Breast pumps. *Journal of Human Lactation* 12(4): 273–274.

Vasquez, J. (2010). Chicana mothering in the 21st century. In O'Reilly, A. (ed.), *Twenty-first-century motherhood: Experience, identity, policy, agency*. New York, NY: Columbia University Press, pp. 23–39.

Victora, C. G., Bahl, R., Barros, A. J., França, G. V., Horton, S., Krasevec, J., Murch, S., Sankar, M. J., Walker, N., Rollins, N. C. and The Lancet Breastfeeding Series Group. (2016). Breastfeeding in the 21st century: Epidemiology, mechanisms, and lifelong effect. *The Lancet* 387(10017): 475–490.

Voss, S. (2017). Go girl. *The Guardian Weekend Supplement*, 4 May, 16–22.

Waight, E. (2014). Second-hand consumption among middle-class mothers in the UK: Thrift, distinction and risk. *Families, Relationships and Societies* 3(1): 159–162.

Waitt, G. and Harada, T. (2016). Parenting, care and the family car. *Social & Cultural Geography* 17(8): 1079–1100.

Waldby, C. and Mitchell, R. (2006). *Tissue economies: Blood, organs and cell lines in late capitalism*. Durham, NC and London, UK: Duke University Press.

Walker, L. and Cavanagh, S. (1999). Women's Design Service: Feminist resources for urban environments. In Rothschild, J. (ed.), *Design and Feminism: Revisioning spaces, places and everyday things*. New Brunswick, NJ: Rutgers, pp. 149–158.

Warner, J. (2006). *Perfect madness: Motherhood in the age of anxiety*. London, UK: Penguin.

Warner, J. (2009). 'Ban the Breastpump'. *New York Times*, 2 April, available at http://opinionator.blogs.nytimes.com/2009/04/02/why-i-dumped-the-pump/ (accessed 12 September 2012).

Watkins, M. (2011). Teachers' tears and the affective geography of the classroom. *Emotion, Space and Society* 4(3): 137–143.

Watson, S. (2006). *City publics: The (dis) enchantments of urban encounters*. Oxon, UK: Routledge.

Weir, A. (2005). Global universal caregiver. *Constellations* 12(3): 308–330.

Weisman, L. (1994). *Discrimination by design: A feminist critique of the man-made environment*. Champaign-Urbana, IL: University of Illinois Press.

Wekerle, G. (2004). Framing feminist claims for urban citizenship. In Staehleli, L., Kofman, E. and Peake, L. (eds.), *Mapping women, making politics: Feminist perspectives on political geography*. New York, NY: Routledge, pp. 245–260.

Whatmore, S. J. (2006). Materialist returns: Practising cultural geography in and for a more-than-human world. *Cultural Geographies* 13(4): 600–609.

Whatmore, S. J. (2013). Earthly powers and affective environments: An ontological politics of flood risk. *Theory, Culture & Society* 30(7–8): 33–50.

White, A. (2007). Applebee's: Cooking up breastfeeding trouble. *Blisstree*, available at http://www.blisstree.com/breastfeeding123/applebees-cooking-up-breastfeeding-trouble (accessed 24 July 2009).

Williamson, I., Leeming, D., Lyttle, S. and Johnson, S. (2012). 'It should be the most natural thing in the world': Exploring first-time mothers' breastfeeding difficulties in the UK using audio-diaries and interviews. *Maternal & Child Nutrition* 8(4): 434–447.

Wilson, E. (1991). *Sphinx in the city: Urban life, the control of disorder and women.* London, UK: Virago.

Wilson, E. (1992). The invisible flâneur. *New Left Review* 191: 90–110.

Wolf, J. (2006) What feminists can do for breastfeeding and what breastfeeding can do for feminists. *Signs* 31(2): 397–424.

World Health Organization. (2002). Infant and young child nutrition: Global strategy on infant and young child feeding, 16 April, available at http://apps.who.int/gb/archive/pdf_files/WHA55/ea5515.pdf (accessed 15 February 2010).

World Health Organization. (2003). *Global strategy for infant and young child feeding.* Geneva, Switzerland: World Health Organization.

World Health Organization. (2011). Breastfeeding for six months best for babies everywhere. Available at http://www.who.int/mediacentre/news/statements/2011/breastfeeding_20110115/en/ (accessed 20 August 2012).

Wridt, P. (2010). A qualitative GIS approach to mapping urban neighborhoods with children to promote physical activity and child-friendly community planning. *Environment & Planning B: Planning & Design* 37(1): 129–147.

Wright, M. (2005). The paradoxes of protests: The Mujeres de Negro of Northern Mexico. *Gender, Place and Culture* 12(3): 277–292.

Young, I. M. (2005). *On female body experience: 'Throwing like a girl' and other essays.* Oxford, UK: Oxford University Press.

Ziegler, F. and Schwanen, T. (2011). 'I like to go out to be energised by different people': An exploratory analysis of mobility and wellbeing in later life. *Ageing and Society* 31(5): 758–781.

Index

activism: citizen, 90, 91; everyday, 84, 90, 122; health, 89, 107, 102; lactation/breastfeeding, 88, 89, 91, 92, 93; maternal, 19; carework, 89, 95, 101, 120

Adey, Peter, 34

advocacy: breastfeeeding/lactation, 8, 88, 90, 91, 93–96, 101–102; maternal, 112; parenting, 1

affect/affects, 2, 4, 12, 33–36, 46, 48, 50–52, 54, 60, 67, 69, 74, 77, 79–80, 85, 108–109, 113, 115, 119–120

'affect alien', 67–68, 79, 80

affective atmospheres/environments, 46, 49–50, 60

agency/agentic mothers, 59; babies, 6, 23, 49, 121; breastmilk, 53–54, 59, 61; matter, 48, 53–54, 55, 58, 61

agential intra-action, 5, 57, 63

Ahmed, Sara, 47, 67–68, 70, 77–80, 83–85

Aitken, Stuart, 3, 6, 19, 61, 95

Alaimo, Stacy, 4, 33–35, 57

Andrews, Gavin, 74, 90, 94

anti-consumerism, 42

assemblage, 36–37, 39; breastfeeding, 53, 55, 59–61, 63–64, 90;

mother-baby, 33–34, 40–46, 49–51; parenting, 40

austerity, 121

Baby Friendly Initiative, 71, 86, 90, 102, 103

Barad, Karen, 4–5, 36–37, 43, 47, 53, 57

Baraitser, Lisa, 18, 21, 29, 35–36, 39–41, 45, 53

Barett, Carla, 121

Bartlett, Alison, 8, 54–55, 64, 73, 91, 93, 106–107, 112

becoming, 22–24, 26–27, 29–31, 57, 119; maternal, 17–18, 21–22, 33; mobile, 22, 35–36, 41–42, 120

Bennett, Jane, 61

birth, 7–9, 20–22, 45, 59, 111; prebirth, 28, 29, 108; postbirth, 12, 18, 25, 34, 54, 61, 63, 71–72, 76, 88, 102, 106, 109; trauma, 50

Bissell, David, 34, 41, 44–45

blocked ducts, 11, 54, 59, 61–64

Blum, Linda, 106, 107

body boundary, 55, 61, 68, 73, 107–108

Boswell-Penc, Maia, 15, 89, 104, 108–104, 114

Bourantani, Eleni, 15, 121

Bowlby, Sophie, 5

About the Author

Kate Boyer is a Senior Lecturer of human geography in the School of Geography and Planning at Cardiff University in the UK. She received her PhD in human geography in 2001 from McGill University in Montreal, Canada, and over the past ten years has written extensively about issues of motherhood, politics and space. She has published this research in journals such as *Progress in Human Geography*; *Environment and Planning D: Society and Space*; *Gender, Place and Culture*; *Social and Cultural Geography* and *Feminist Theory*. She has also shared her work with infant-feeding practitioners and policymakers through the auspices of a bridge-building seminar series funded by the Economic and Social Research Council which ran over 2015 and 2016 (with Drs Sally Dowling and David Pontin). In 2016 she presented her research to the UK Houses of Parliament through the All-Party Parliamentary Group on Infant Feeding and Inequality, and her work has also been noted in the Welsh National Assembly. Born in the US and having lived in both the US and Canada, she currently lives in Bristol with her partner and school-age son.

Lightning Source UK Ltd.
Milton Keynes UK
UKHW01f2118220818
327639UK00001B/90/P